T0068244

BREAKING
THE
CURSE

The Revitalization of a
Dying Contentious Church

JONATHAN KINNER

WESTBOW
P R E S S®
A DIVISION OF THOMAS NELSON
& ZONDERVAN

WestBow Press books may be ordered through booksellers or by contacting:

WestBow Press
A Division of Thomas Nelson & Zondervan
1663 Liberty Drive
Bloomington, IN 47403
www.westbowpress.com
844-714-3454

Scripture quotations marked (MEV) are taken from THE HOLY BIBLE, MODERN ENGLISH VERSION. Copyright© 2014 by Military Bible Association. Published and distributed by Charisma House.

Scripture marked (NKJV) taken from the New King James Version®. Copyright © 1982 by Thomas Nelson. Used by permission. All rights reserved.

Scripture marked (KJV) taken from the King James Version of the Bible.

ISBN: 978-1-6642-5678-1 (sc)
ISBN: 978-1-6642-5679-8 (hc)
ISBN: 978-1-6642-5677-4 (e)

Library of Congress Control Number: 2022902129

Print information available on the last page.

WestBow Press rev. date: 2/10/2022

This book is dedicated to my beautiful
wife for the love and support
she has always given me in both the good times and hard times.

I am deeply grateful for the work of the Lord in our lives
and the lives of our churches, He truly is the Good Shepherd.

I am thankful for all the members of my
church that stuck with me and saw
the process of revitalization through breaking the
curse of contention in our body of believers.

CONTENTS

INTRODUCTION

"Pastor, they said they were going to eat you for lunch."
I knew then that I might be seeing the
end of my time at the church.

You are most likely reading this book because you are pastoring a church that has a history of contention, or you are praying about taking a church that is known for conflict. Most likely, you wonder how the church will survive, like a sinking ship, and you feel you can do nothing to stop it. I want to encourage you that it is entirely possible to walk with a church through the difficulties of contention with a little bit of wisdom and a lot of patience. There are many books with different approaches to revitalizing dying churches; however, there are those churches that have a history of contention and have failed numerous revitalization efforts. These churches are not just dying, but there are characteristics in these churches that are driving them into the ground.

When the church hired me, I knew it had a history of contention and was known for its departures- sometimes significant. It had short pastor tenures where the pastors of the last few decades had left because of a certain level of contention while endeavoring to revitalize this church. The church was facing its end, and I had a year and a half to two years to turn it around before closing the doors. One of the misconceptions about these churches is that they are full of hateful people. These churches are often full of good people with a small group that causes the bulk of contention.

People run from conflict, and understandably so, strife creates an environment toxic to spiritual and numerical growth.

The goal of this book is not to turn an awful church into a good church but to lead a good church out of the swamp of contention that is drowning it. Ultimately, your goal is even to help those who are contentious move forward into a healthier church culture that will allow the church to gain some traction in its work for eternity. As long as Satan creates wars within the church, he knows that the church will not fight him outside.

Jesus knew their thoughts and said to them, "Every kingdom divided against itself is brought to desolation. And every city or house divided against itself will not stand."[1]

One of the most prominent reasons that contentious churches stay within their four walls is their regular drama. Pastors and congregations are worn out not by the wars outside the church but the wars waged inside the church. This condition keeps their focus on putting out fires and expends their energy, time, and emotional/relational resources. It creates an environment that repels people and keeps its congregants from inviting others into it. War in the church is ugly and has eternal consequences, which begs the question: Is there a way to navigate the contentious church and turn it around for Jesus? I believe the answer is yes, and this book will help flesh that out.

In full disclosure, about two years after we navigated the contentious time at our church, I started to write this book. Eventually, I passed the baton to another pastor who is currently pastoring the church and is building on the groundwork we laid the years I was at the church. I hesitated to publish this book due to this transition. Still, if Jesus can use my experiences for His Kingdom and I can help other followers of Jesus bring purity, unity, and vision to their churches, I will gladly do so.

---

[1] Matthew 12:25 MEV

CHAPTER ONE

Let Me Talk You Out of It

B efore I go into what it will take to revitalize a contentious church, I want to do for you what was done for me before joining the church: try to talk you out of it. I know this may seem counterintuitive to the point of this book, but I would not be honest without first informing you of the risks you may encounter in this task. Many denominations are steering away from revitalizing dying churches with a history of contention, and instead are planting their replacements. Why would they do that when there is already a good church in this town? That is what I thought. However, I want to give you a few reasons to reconsider revitalizing that contentious dying church.

1. The church hasn't taken responsibility for what is killing it

When you are weighing and praying about the opportunity to revitalize this church, take some time to learn its history. Ask for an information sheet on the church, call its former pastors, ask lots of questions, and learn who the major players are.

Churches in these situations usually have reoccurring problems that have plagued them over the years, and the church members have turned a blind eye. Most people hate confrontation and want to get along with everybody, so they slide on the parameters of God because that could spur contention from the people they care about. Thus, the vetting process of leaders is generalized, the confrontation of sin in the church is skipped, and the problems persist as the congregation waits for the next pastor to "fix" the situation. Unfortunately, the new pastor walks in on this situation and attempts to broach the elephant in the room, and the congregation sits back as a new target has been created on his back.

2. Their motivations are less than ideal

Let me ask you some questions. What motivates you? What motivates them? Why do you serve? Why do they serve? These questions are fundamental to have answered before you take on the church. The truth is, opportunity finds its way to those who are seeking, asking, knocking, and serving. Jesus has a way of rewarding obedience with further opportunity to be obedient.

Regarding church, if a congregation is passionate about the gospel, has their eyes on serving Jesus, and loves those around them, why don't they act? Why do they sit back and wait for the next "savior" to step into their church and save it from dying? Because their motivation is their institution, not the kingdom. Biblically, the church is the vehicle for the gospel to be preached among the nations so the kingdom of God can grow. In these circumstances, the gospel is the vehicle to grow their church, and success has more to do with their institution than God's kingdom.

How can you find out what a church's motivation is? Answer these four questions:

- What values do they advocate for?
- What values do they make decisions with?

- What values do they break fellowship over?
- What values move them into action?

Unfortunately, any action is not good enough. The motivation behind their activity must be correct. If their cause is centered on their traditions, preservation, the past, or even their facilities, you will find that Jesus will counter some of those motivations and will hit a wall.

3. They can be a swamp of poor culture

I have repeatedly seen a young family taking on a dying church to walk into a toxic culture that taxes the new pastor and his family. Can I say that this is very important for your wife? I didn't realize the pain she would feel witnessing her husband being the target of regular criticism and attacking privately and publicly. I genuinely believe it was harder on her than me.

These situations will turn your children off from following Christ. Your family is much more vital than you trying to save a dying institution. My children were too young enough to see the worst of it, but I was embarrassed for the church members who acted out so poorly. The key in these situations is to feed the healthy culture and not to cater to the unhealthy culture, as you will read later in the book.

4. They don't genuinely love their community

My position is that God has a purpose for a church being in a particular community. He put them as a light on a hill for those people. However, in many of these situations, the church becomes convinced that it is their community's job to serve them and not the other way around. The church is put together to be a blessing and not just receive a blessing. In some of these situations, the church is primarily motivated by self-advancement. Essentially, we will love those who have loved us first.

A church that is not fueled by a love for their community will not grow the right way, even if they grow. I recall Paul's groaning as he walked into Athens in Acts 17:16. When we serve the Lord, He will give us a heart for those around us, for the deceptions they have bought into, for the habits that bind them, and for the sin that entangles them. This heart is probably what brought you to this church; however, if a church doesn't love those in the community and is motivated only by institutional advancement, you will find it hard to keep Jesus at the center. If the lost state of the community doesn't affect them, but a pep rally to fill their pews does, there is something terribly wrong.

5. It may not be God's church at all

One of the most shocking statements I ever heard a church member say was along the lines of, "This is our church, and you will run it our way." Really? I thought this was God's church where Christ is the Head. I am just going to say it: Many times, a church is more of an expression of the people and culture than the God they claim to worship. Jesus has become a personal image that takes on whatever form they see fit and expresses their imagination more than revelation found in scripture.

Some may say this is judgmental, but if the Jesus found in scripture is subverted by the Jesus they worship, they are not the same person. Jesus becomes a slave to a personal ideology, and only where the Jesus of scripture and their imagination intersect is what they will accept. If they don't hear the words of Jesus, then they won't hear your words when you speak Jesus' words. This completely breaks my heart when people who claim to follow Jesus reject His words and substitute them with something more generic and self-defined.

6. Churches have lifespans just like people

Think of the transient nature of your life. You get a measly eighty years on earth, and then your life is over. You could say the same about churches. Not a single church (local assembly) has perpetual historical existence. Not to be confused with the perpetual presence of the true church through time. Every congregation has a period it serves and aids the coming generation. Once the next generation steps up, the former must pass the baton and enter eternity.

As a pastor recently told me, "It's not about a name, institution or personal legacy but that the next generation would carry forward the true faith and continue the work for Jesus." A huge problem arises when a church refuses to pass that baton and feels the younger generation should carry forward the personal legacy of an institution and not the faith once for all delivered to the saints. Perseverance of the faith is replaced by the preservation of a system that has more to do with the institution than the God it served.

7. Weigh the risks you may be walking into

We live in a day when churches are not just gatherings of people but recognized public institutions that can be sued, go bankrupt, have extraordinary insurance claims, and see moral and ethical abuse or even criminal charges. When you enter this church, you will be responsible for those risks. I am sure you have the best intentions, and there will always be some risk in life, but if you enter a situation that places you or your family at excessive risk, you may want to reconsider entering that ministry. Whatever moral or legal abuses you experience must be dealt with and reported to the appropriate authorities.

8. Be careful with who you entrust
yourself and your family

My last point is this: Your family means something. There is a
tremendous turnover rate for kids raised in the church, especially
pastor kids. Jesus didn't entrust Himself to just anyone (John 2:24).
What you participate in will be construed as what you believe
to be biblical Christianity to your kids. Too often, we will enter
non-biblical Christian situations for the sake of ministry and the
price of our families. We will tolerate all kinds of idolatry and non-
Christian behavior and motivations for the sake of the ministry. I
mean, that's what Jesus would do, right? Wrong.

Jesus and His apostles called idolaters, sinners, and false
religious systems to repentance and obedience to the true faith.
In the twenty-first century, we have relaxed so much on what
we call Christian that many honestly have stopped evaluating
our institutions and movements through the lens of scripture. If
a church is dying and you must aid an institution that has lost its
Christian distinction, it's better to walk in and call it to repentance
and fulfill God's ministry elsewhere.

Conclusion

I know this chapter has a negative tone, but that is not my
intention. However, I do not feel we should substitute reality
for a pipedream in the name of Jesus. The truth is, taking on a
church dying by contention will be the hardest thing you will do,
and I believe that you as a minister should reconsider what you are
willing to risk in taking it. Please be in prayer and keep in mind that
you were called to serve Christ for His kingdom, not the personal
agenda of those who have ulterior motives or ambitions.

If you decide to take on a contentious church facing death,
know that you have the privilege to serve as a representative of

Jesus, in love leading the church forward to health. You also have the responsibility to operate your office according to His Word to fulfill His Will in His church. You will lose people in this process, who you will continue to love even if they leave. Let God handle the consequences; you be faithful to fulfill your ministry.

> *I charge thee therefore before God, and the Lord Jesus Christ,*
> *who shall judge the quick and the dead at*
> *his appearing and his kingdom;*
> *preach the word; be instant in season, out of season; reprove,*
> *rebuke, exhort with all longsuffering and doctrine.*
> *For the time will come when they will not endure sound doctrine;*
> *but after their own lusts shall they heap to*
> *themselves teachers, having itching ears;*
> *and they shall turn away their ears from the*
> *truth, and shall be turned unto fables.*
> *But watch thou in all things, endure afflictions,*
> *do the work of an evangelist,*
> *make full proof of thy ministry.*[2]

---

[2] 2 Timothy 4:1-5 KJV

CHAPTER TWO

The Reality of Sin in the Contentious Church

If I haven't talked you out of taking the church yet, let me continue by dealing with the reality of the sins of contention in the church. The truth is, I have to. This is not to steer you away from reading this book but as an encouragement that you can be a channel of new life in a contentious church. Some sins are considered heinous in our churches and will not be tolerated, like adultery, fornication, homosexuality, and the like. Unfortunately, other sins are just as heinous, but they are justified in the church, and a blind eye is often turned to such behavior for the sake of peace and feeling intimidated by those who commit them. These sins cause so much damage to the body of believers, but because they are socially tolerated, or the people who practice them are feared, few call it out.

Picture this with me; let's say you are asked to pastor a church. The people are friendly, and they want you to come to their church. They are very religious, but you find out that the associate pastor is cheating on his wife, and the church knows about it but doesn't want to hurt his feelings. You find out that multiple couples live together unmarried, and some hold leadership in the church. The women are lewd, and the men exercise no self-control. On top of that, they've decided to allow other faiths in (to be open-minded), and sometimes they get drunk or high because they want to win those who live in such ways. When pastors in the past tried to deal with these issues scripturally, they were shut down.

Would you take the church?

Most would tell you no. The scenario that I just created is only about half of the deeds of the flesh listed in Galatians 5. You need to know that religion is often used as a mask to cover sin, and tradition is deceptively satisfying to the religious mind. In the list of the deeds of the flesh found in Galatians 5, we all could remember those deeds of the flesh that our culture defines as sinful but let me also include the deeds of the flesh that are often overlooked. This list will be referenced throughout the book as you read through it:

hatred, strife, jealousy, rage, selfishness, dissensions, heresies, envy,[3]

- Hatred: Strong Negative Reaction; a feeling toward someone considered an enemy, possibly indicating volatile hostility.[4]
    o Not agreeing with someone may lead to rejection or even parting ways. Still, hatred is revealed in active hostility to bring the demise of their adversary, stain their reputation, or even character assassination.
- Strife: This means those who practice strife quarrel, especially rivalry, contention, and wrangling.[5]
    o This is the competing nature of the fleshly mind. It finds its source in the ego of someone who refuses

---

[3] Galatians 5:20b-21a MEV
[4] McWilliams, Warren 2003. "Hate, Hatred." In The Holman Illustrated Bible Dictionary, 723. Nashville: Holman Bible Publishers.
[5] Vine, W. E. 1981. "Strife." In The Vine's Expository Dictionary of Old and New Testament Words. Volume 4, 82. Old Tappan: Fleming H. Revell.

to lose and is determined to win against opponents. It views others as contenders to be conquered, not congregants for cooperation.

- Jealousy: which means to be jealous and zeal.[6]
  - o This fuels hostility when someone feels that someone else has an advantage and vigorously attempts to remove it.
- Rage: Hot anger and passion[7]
  - o This one explains itself.
- Selfishness: This word denotes ambition, self-seeking, rivalry, self-will being the underlying idea in the word; hence it denotes party-making. It is derived from erithos, meaning they will seek and win followers and create factions and sects.[8]
  - o This word points to the motives of the rivalry, that being, as some translations translate it, selfish ambition. This is the case when someone is convinced that they will have their way, forms parties or sects, and attempts to divide the group and bolster their cause against the group they disagree with. This can lead to my side vs. your side instead of our side being God's side.
- Dissensions: literally division or standing apart or putting asunder.[9]
  - o This is the mentality of "them or us," as described later in the book when the divisive individual has caused division. It is when a person is unwilling to embrace another group and divides themselves and others from them.

---

[6] Vine, W. E. 1981. "Jealous." In The Vine's Expository Dictionary of Old and New Testament Words. Volume 2, 273. Old Tappan: Fleming H. Revell.
[7] Vine, W. E. 1981. "Wrath." In The Vine's Expository Dictionary of Old and New Testament Words. Volume 4, 239. Old Tappan: Fleming H. Revell.
[8] Vine, W. E. 1981. "Faction." In The Vine's Expository Dictionary of Old and New Testament Words. Volume 2, 68. Old Tappan: Fleming H. Revell.
[9] Vine, W. E. 1981. "Sedition." In The Vine's Expository Dictionary of Old and New Testament Words. Volume 3, 336. Old Tappan: Fleming H. Revell.

- <u>Heresies:</u> denotes a choosing, choice. Then, that which is chosen, and hence, an opinion, especially a self-willed opinion, which is substituted for submission to the power of truth leads to division and the formations of sects. Such erroneous opinions are frequently the outcome of personal preference or the prospect of advantage. Which often leads to ruin.[10]
  - o When we think of heresies, we think of people of opposing doctrine, but actual heresy comes from those who have refused to submit to the truth revealed in scripture, create a truth of their liking, and causes a divide over the truth they have made that has very little to do with the truth found in scripture. These "heresies" are usually found in designing religion for personal preference over biblical truth, and yes, this can be found in the liberal and traditional camps.
- <u>Envy:</u> is the feeling of displeasure produced by witnessing or hearing of the advantage or prosperity of others; an evil sense is always attached to this word.[11]
  - o This is the feeling that will cause good people to do bad things. When they feel someone has an advantage over them, they decide to bring the other person down instead of making themselves better.

The list above should create three thoughts within you. The first should be the times that you have been guilty of such fleshly activity. We are human and sinners; we all can be guilty of acting in the flesh at times of pressure or strong fleshly emotion. You will need to curb these desires in the Spirit of God and ask God to grant you control as you deal with these sins in the contentious church.

---

[10] Vine, W. E. 1981. "Heresy." In The Vine's Expository Dictionary of Old and New Testament Words. Volume 2, 217. Old Tappan: Fleming H. Revell.
[11] Vine, W. E. 1981. "Envy." In The Vine's Expository Dictionary of Old and New Testament Words. Volume 2, 37. Old Tappan: Fleming H. Revell.

If you do not have the self-control of your reactions, a controversial church will push you over the edge, and you will become part of the problem. If you have a habit of these sins in your life, repent now and reel these in. You need to find men of high spiritual stamina and ask for accountability, do it now!

The second thought is that you feel that connecting these sins to people in your church makes you sick to your stomach. It should. You may even sense that we should never judge those around us in such ways but understand that righteous judgment is not blind to the sins in the church, nor does it condemn those in the church, but looks for restoration. You need to be able to lovingly discern the sins killing your church, the people who exercise those sins, and the proper response to those sins. Ignoring the sins of a drug addict will never help them or those around them; the same goes for the corruption in the church. In making this discernment, understand that people will make mistakes at times. You are looking for patterns of these contentious activities that have habitually plagued the church.

The third thought is, does this make them bad people? The answer is no. Just because someone is participating in sinful activity that is destroying their church doesn't mean that they are awful people. Some of the kindest people I know are those who allow sin to destroy their lives. They are friendly, capable of love, and often have good values. However, our culture in the church has caused us to differentiate between people of moral sin vs. conscience sin, the sins committed with the hands and eye vs. the sins of the tongue. We will point out the error of the drug addict, homosexual or alcoholic while ignoring the corruption of a seared conscience and a rebellious heart even in our midst.

If a church is willing to preach and discipline sin in the moral spectrum of Christianity but turns a blind eye to the sins listed above, that is why these remain in the church and cause so much damage. We have a certain tolerance for these behaviors, believing them to be less critical or misunderstood. Still, I think in the eyes of our Shepherd, these are viewed as worse because they infiltrate and divide His body of believers which is the primary concern of the apostles in Acts 20:28-38; Romans 16:17; 1 Corinthians 3:3; 2 Corinthians 12:19-21; 2 Timothy 3:1-5; James 1:26,3:1-12; Jude 1:19. These sins find a place in the church because people are scared to be the target of such sins and remain silent. The pastor who decides to take these on will bear the brunt of the wrath of these sins.

These behaviors have found some churches very comfortable because they are not as apparent as the moral sins but just as destructive. These church practices have destroyed the reputation of churches and ministers, run good churches into the ground, and destroyed some ministers' ministries. Some have counted these churches as lost and let them die, but some are willing to step up and lead churches from a fragrance of death to life, from a culture of toxicity to peace, and from a ministry of dishonor to that of honor. If you have found yourself in the midst of or entering a church where these sins are present, this book will aid you as you serve your Shepherd in His flock to bring it back in alignment with Him and His Word. I pray that you find wisdom and insight from this book that will aid you in leading your flock to the green pastures and still waters of Jesus.

Before we dive into the substance of this book, I want to encourage you to do the hard work now. To read, study and apply the scriptures to your church. Because of the political environment, many pastors have been put in between the bible and their church members and their position as pastors. The issue for today is not to only bring these churches back under the Word of God but to continue to build them according to the scriptures, or some young pastor 40 years from now will be dealing with the same problems you are facing today. Don't make the mistakes of previous pastors that just kicked the contentious can down the road to the next generation of preachers. When my children grow up and come to an age where they are called upon to serve the Lord, I pray that I did my part to faithfully serve my Lord and hand down a ministry to their generation that pleases Him and will not become a nightmare for the next generation of the Lord's servants, where they have to fix problems I was too cowardly to address.

I believe here is an excellent place to inform you of a psychological concept that will help explain why a church gives a pass to their own culture while criticizing the culture around them for the same corruption. To provide you with an example, I was amazed when I was scrolling through a social media platform to see one of the ladies from my church rant about the corruption in our government. It's not that she was wrong, for she was exactly right! We were witnessing tremendous corruption in our political world. The appalling part was that she had watched the exact kind of corruption in our church but was silent about it and not only that but saw no reason to deal with it.

What makes people hold two standards? One for their inner circle of peers and one for the outside culture around us. The concept is that of tribalism. In our effort to build churches and grow Christ's Kingdom in many ways, we have settled for building religious tribes instead of churches. I have found that there are eight primary reasons for this:

1. Tribes are easier to build than churches because the gospel has become more of an initiatory procedure for the tribe going to heaven instead of a life-altering commitment to Christ.
2. Tribes share more common social/political/economic structures and cultures, where churches aim to live beyond such systems and bring all into the Kingdom of Christ.
3. Tribes are social instead of communal, much like social media, where a social shell dominates honest relationships.
4. Tribes promote tribal commitment where churches promote Christ's commitment shared by the community of believers.

5. Tribes choose leaders based on who best represents and promotes the tribe, not the scriptural mandates, where a church will aim to have leaders that reflect the divine decrees.

6. Tribes operate by cultural and ethical norms set by a base culture that keeps the tribe intact, where a church will conform its culture and ethics to the teachings of scripture, putting unity in the context of purity.

7. Tribes can be dominated by extra-biblical structures such as economic status, social and political allegiances, race, traditions, cultural norms, hobbies, etc. The church is formed based on Christ and holds to a biblical culture, and brings all other structures, cultures, and allegiances into subjection to the teachings of Christ and His apostles.

8. Tribes carry two sets of ethical standards, one for those inside the tribe (more lenient and overlooking of sin), and another for those outside the tribe (stricter and more critical.) Where a church will be concerned with the ethics of their own body being understanding but not overlooking sin seeking recovery and more gracious with those who are "outside."

I am convinced that we have been building religious tribes in many ways, not churches. When you are in a church, there will always be a few common threads that run through the tapestry of that congregation. A church should constantly evaluate that those threads remain an allegiance to Jesus, adhere to the Sacred Scriptures, and regularly aim to subject any tribal instinct that threatens the church's purity in her commitment to Christ.

CHAPTER THREE

Where to Start: Do Your Homework

If you are reading this, I assume I couldn't talk you out of it. Good, may God be with you and guide you in leading this church back to biblical faithfulness. When my wife and I decided to join our church plant to an existing church, we were nervous. We had been approached before by this church and turned them down over concerns of the controversy in their history, and our church plant was doing well. Now, the future of the ministry the Lord had brought us to was in the hands of this other body of believers. At the same time, they knew that the future of their church was in the hands of this new pastor and wife. This church had quick pastor rotation and had a reputation in the community for being a "fighting church"[12] with regular departures. Growing up, I had been a part of a church that went through a split because of a pastor trying to revitalize our church. I knew that this was going to be a difficult journey but always hoped that this existing church would mesh well with our church plant to see our community reached with the gospel and a solid biblical church established. While on this journey, I came up with the 15 commitments for a

---

[12] Not my own assessment but that which I heard from the community.

revitalization pastor that you should read over; the document is resource "A" in the resource section.

We have learned a few things that helped us out tremendously along this journey, and we have made several mistakes that could have been avoided. My hope is by reading this book; you will apply some of the things we learned and avoid making the same mistakes we did. This book doesn't mean that you will have a challenge-free ministry but that you will be able to navigate some of those challenges and come out the other side. All in all, our journey through this process was not uncommon though it felt that we were the only ones in the world who were going through this. By the grace of God, we were able to move the church forward and do what the previous pastors wanted to do but were prohibited. Let's look at a good place to start and give you some traction in moving the church forward. This book is not an island, so please read other books on the subject since we all can contribute to church revitalization.

Let me start this chapter with a challenge. Great men and strong men have failed at this task. Many believe that revitalization can occur with enough patience and political diplomacy. Still, I am concerned that many in this camp would have disapproved of Jesus' relationship with the Pharisees, Paul's exhortations to Timothy and Titus about dealing with Ephesus and Crete's problems. Many will celebrate the reformers of old then condemn the person today with not having enough patience or political tact who is dealing with very similar issues, if not the same. The problem with our distance from the past causes us to laud men of the past for their bravery, and we will critique such courage today in the face of very similar challenges. I am convinced that many of the issues that Jesus faced, the apostles met, and the reformers faced are still alive today and are killing our churches. Remember Paul's exhortation in 1 Corinthians 16:13-14 MEV

> "Watch, stand fast in the faith, be bold like men, and be
> strong. Let all that you do be done with love."

You must remember that it is not you that will save this church; God will. The most important habit you should get into is intercession. Revitalization is not the work of a convention or an association trying to save their institutions but God giving this church another chance to repent before He takes out their candlestick. You, like Moses in Numbers 14, should intercede for the church and beg God to give the church another chance and not take their candlestick. You, as the pastor, are an intercessor between the church and God. You, as the pastor, are a prophet that warns the people to turn back to the ways of God and leave behind vain things that are of no profit, you as the pastor are Christ's under-shepherd to lead the church to good pasture, life-giving water, and sometimes will have to protect the fold. You have to be faithful to do your part; as long as you do that, the church's response is between them and God.

As for you: When walking into these institutions, the first thing you need to do is commit to being the servant of God that He wants you to be. I would encourage you to commit 2 Timothy 2:22-26 to memory because you will be brought to a crossroads that will either lead to health or death with each occurring situation. Revitalization of a contentious church is not in making a few good significant decisions in a short amount of time but a pattern of good choices in the small and large situations you will face.

> *So flee youthful desires and pursue righteousness, faith, love, and peace with those who call on the Lord out of a pure heart. But avoid foolish and unlearned debates, knowing that they create strife. The servant of the Lord must not quarrel, but must be gentle toward all people, able to teach, patient, in gentleness instructing those in opposition.*[13]

---

[13] 2 Timothy 2:22-25a MEV

Timothy is to flee immature desires and passions to pursue godliness with those who walk in integrity with the scriptures and avoid those who cause strife by disputes (contentions). Why? Because the servant of the Lord must not strive (quarrel, fight) but remain gentle while not bending the truth but teaching it. We do not give in to the demands of those given to strife but gently correct and instruct them from the inerrant, unchanging word of God. We join ourselves with others who call on the Lord out of a pure heart. Those in your church who call on the Lord out of a pure heart, let them become your focus. We often make the mistake of turning our attention to the contentious, but we should focus our attention on the healthy and instruct the contentious to join in, too, instead of allowing the controversial to poison the rest of the body and drain us. At the same time, understanding that these people are not just opposing you but themselves, they are hurting themselves as much as anyone else.

> Perhaps God will grant them repentance to know the truth, and they may escape from the snare of the devil, after being captured by him to do his will.[14]

Their acceptance of the truth is not in your bending it to fit their demands but God working in them to acknowledge it. A faithful pastor will not bow but gently instruct these people while joining those of a pure heart. Paul brings out the truth about these individuals that the devil captures them as an instrument of hostility and division in the church. Now, I know that it is politically incorrect to say that. Still, the hostility you will face will be very real. If you take the approach that you are in denial about the reality of the situation and the condition of the church, you will not act wisely and be like a blind man trying to navigate a minefield.

---

[14] 2 Timothy 2:25b-26 MEV

Survey the spiritual landscape: appreciate and evaluate

The first thing you need to focus on is understanding the spiritual landscape of your church. For illustration, my wife and I are inheriting some land, and we want to establish a retreat center on the property. So, we walked the property and discussed the strengths of the type of land (very hilly with a small portion of flat ground) and figured out how to work out or around its weaknesses to accomplish our goal. Churches are similar in that when you enter a church for the first time, there are obvious things about the spiritual landscape you can see, but there are hidden things that are not so obvious that you will one day encounter. The better you understand this landscape, the better you will navigate it, predict difficulty, and see it become fruitful.

This is a crucial part of church revitalization, especially contentious churches; please don't skip it. If you don't understand the history, strengths, weaknesses, and patterns of the church you are in, you will find it almost impossible to navigate through the difficulties you run into. You will never be able to predict every problematic situation, but having a basic understanding of what has kept the church from revitalization in the past will help you overcome those barriers to achieve revitalization in the future. This can be achieved through various means.

Test the temperature

Take an anonymous survey of the church. This will only yield partial results, but you will better understand where most of the congregation is and some hidden tensions that may exist. The first survey I ever asked the church to fill out can be found in the resources portion of this book as resource "B."

Have lots of conversations

In church revitalization, you are not removing the past. You, as a revitalizer, can appreciate definite elements of the past. Listen to the stories of those who brought the church up to this point. Listen with an attentive ear to the sacrifices people made and the church's history. In this process, you will need to appreciate what they have done, but you need to help them look ahead instead of behind, using the past as a launching point to move into the future. I emphasized that the best way to honor the past of this ministry was to make sure this ministry had a future. I found the church's original mission statement, and it almost lined up perfectly with the new mission statement. I encouraged our people to go back to that original mission and move forward in the reason the church was started and to not lose focus on the purpose the church existed.

A second way to grow in your understanding is to talk to members who have been there the longest. This is a mistake that I made. We had two wonderful individuals that were founding members of the church and looking back; I should have spent more time with them just enjoying a cup of coffee and having a conversation about the church. I am sure that I would have avoided some issues if I had just sat down and listened to the church's history from the perspective of two people who had seen it all.

Talk to the rest of the people, ask questions like what brought you to this church? What about this church do you love the most? What are areas do you think could be improved on to see it grow? Why did the previous pastors leave? What should the new pastor know to be successful and faithful at ministering to this church?

Talk to previous pastors and find out why they left the church and what they would tell future pastors about the spiritual terrain of the church and what they would have done the same, and what they would have done differently. I would also have your wife talk to their wife. During the controversy that ensued while at our church, we sat down with a previous pastor and his wife to get counsel on the situation "in confidence," and I watched as his wife and my wife embraced each other and wept because of the struggles they both shared at the church. We, too, mourned over the difficulties at the church, and I believe it was healing in both of our marriages.

Talk to the prominent influencers in the church. They will give you good indicators of what happened with previous pastors and the relationship strife, not that you take what they say as gospel truth. Still, you can understand how they handle pastors they have struggled with and what they find appropriate behavior (both personally and politically) when there is friction. I found these conversations very eye-opening; they prepared me for what may come and what to look for when they had decided to remove a pastor. I was even told the first couple of weeks of my pastorate that I was "walking on thin ice" by looking up definitions of terms of our constitution in Robert's Rules of Order, so I knew the constitution would be a point of contention.

Look for historical markers and patterns

In a church that is dying by contention, usually, the circumstance does not come from a one-time crisis but a long-term pattern of poor decisions, poor relationship practices, poor priorities, and poor politics. Just like when marriages fall apart, homes split, or an individual's life has taken a turn for the worst, it usually comes from long-term patterns. I want to stress that it isn't that these people are bad because these churches are full of well-intentioned people doing what they have always known to do. But, these patterns (sometimes sinful) have developed over the years; they go unchallenged, they get worse, and lead to a church's death. For our church, I put together a basic timeline of the church's history and when specific problems appeared on that timeline with what changes were made during that period of the church's history and the circumstances that led to that change. I also took note of the individuals in those circumstances and the kind of accusations they mounted at the pastors.

Grapple with the historical semantics

This may sound a bit intimidating, but you need to understand the language of the people of your church. One thing that I found when observing the language of the church was that the working definitions that many used in their vocabulary when talking about "church" were different from the working definitions I was using. So, when I said anything, the picture in my mind was different from the picture in their mind. For example, when I said revitalization, they did not get the picture that I had in my mind. Looking back, I wish I would have taken more time to explain my thoughts and even correct definitions that had made their way into the church that did not come from the bible.

If you study hermeneutics, you learn early on about the pretextual biases and presuppositions that we often bring to a text of scripture. The goal of hermeneutics is to remove the lenses of our presuppositions that we may understand the text of scripture without the influence of our own preferential bias and personal baggage. That our understanding is as pure as possible to the thrust and intention of the original author. The same goes for the church; many churches have defined the terms of the bible in specific ways, with certain interpretations that have not always reflected the biblical definitions. So, we err when we think we can go into these churches and use standard Christian language to "lead" our church into revitalization. I know I did. I believe this led to us talking past each other. Trying to correct decades of traditional definitions with the Bible's definitions may lead to more difficulty but is vital in a church that needs revitalization.

We can say the same thing about the constitution. When

working in the church, the constitution was a point of contention, and when I was personally working through it, I found an online resource that provided me with Robert's Rules of Order. Many churches claim to operate by these rules, and ours was no exception, as stated in our constitution. The problem was that the constitution's terms had been traditionally defined around a few individuals' personal views. When I tried to work within the objective definitions, this led to some turmoil.

This is key; you may want to reread this section. You will have to choose carefully at the pace you bring back biblical definitions into a church that its leaders have allowed themselves to redefine biblical, ministerial, and ecclesiastical language with tradition, preference, or personal bias in some cases. Ask them, what is (a) pastor? Deacon? Evangelism? Discipleship? Church? Worship? Ministry? The Bible? The purpose of the church? Whose church is it? The authority of the Bible? What do you mean when you say...?

Start with an informed clean slate

When you research your church to make the most informed, prayer-filled decisions for your church, the information must remain strictly objective. Your love for the people should come from a clean slate, you can't fix the past, and you shouldn't allow it to dictate your feelings toward individuals in the church. You have no basis to know if the information is accurate, and only time will tell what habitual patterns of individuals in your church are real or something they may have already repented from in the past. You need the information to stay watchful and alert to the problems, but do not hold the past against your people. The data is only for objective purposes in dealing with contention, not for confronting the past you had nothing to do with.

CHAPTER FOUR

The Biggest Change a Contentious Church Must Make

———

In a church that is dying by contention, the temptation is to change everything about the church. That is unnecessary, especially in a church known for conflict. The only significant thing at our church that I asked to be changed at this time was the name, for the church had a reputation in the community that we wanted to escape, so we relaunched under a new name. Looking back, I should have waited on this until the contention passed so we could have that clean slate because, sure enough, changing the name didn't change the situation. Other than that, we left the service order, church traditions, and much of the facility intact. My goal was not to rid the church of its heritage but to move it forward and keep it from closing its doors and re-establish it under biblical principles. Contentious churches do not die primarily because of traditional or contemporary services, having older facilities, or if they have pews or chairs. Contentious churches fail mainly because they have an unhealthy church culture that creates an environment toxic to new believers, guests, and, you guessed it, younger families.

This is not only the most significant change that needs to be made but the hardest. When a culture becomes deeply rooted in the church, it can be complex, if not impossible, to uproot. Changing a church culture starts at redefinition. By the way, there will be resistance to redefining the culture of a church. First, let me give you some indicators of your church culture.

- Is the church culture stuck in the past? Often when a church is dying, the conversations will be filled with what has happened, who gave what, who did what, etc. Past events or people will consume them. Your job as a revitalizer is not to rid the church of its past but to focus its eye on the future. You must convince your church that its best days are not behind but ahead. It's not that you do not appreciate what people have done, but you can't live there. Counselors all the time work with people who can't move forward because they're stuck in what their life once was. Churches need that same counsel and need to accept that if they do not look ahead, the days of their church are numbered.

- Are controversies frequent or seldom? A pastor once told me that a church would grow if they could get along. Most church fights are not over the issue at hand but when the issue is handled poorly and causes an escalation of the problem. When variance, emulations, wrath, strife, seditions, gossip, dissension, ultimatums, and even lying becomes a tool to gain political advantage over others, you will have a toxic culture.

- The stability of relationships between church leaders: Churches imitate the strength of their leadership. If you have unstable leaders, they will lead to an unstable church. If you have stable, patient, and cooperative leadership, the church will respect and reflect that.

- The process by which problems are handled: this is a reiteration of the second point. Problems don't have to be nightmares. In my marriage, we have rules for disagreements like "not getting revenge no matter what" to "always be willing to be corrected about a false perception," to "assume the best, not the worst," to "be honest and yielding to the other," and "avoid using exaggerated or inflammatory language." Most problems are minor; they only escalate when those in them handle them poorly and cause more significant issues by their actions outside of the original problem (politics.) This is so important that our new constitution laid out a problem resolution process according to the scriptural design.

- The church's values: Are the church's values aligned with the bible, or is there a separate agenda that has little to do with the bible and more to do with preference. Every church says they value evangelism, but many do not participate. Every church says they want to be biblical but is the bible used? The actual values of the church are those values that are lived out, not just said.

- How does the church handle new people and new ideas? A culture that rejects new people and new ideas that are still within the boundaries of scripture just because "we have never done it that way" will repel new people. New people offer unique insight and a fresh perspective; let's keep our doctrine to the bible.

- How does the church view the word of God? Cultures that aim to be biblical are healthy; cultures that do not find their definition by the bible are not healthy. The bible is a treasure trove of truth and to attempt to operate a church outside of that truth is vain. This goes for both those who try to operate by the "in" method or operate by tradition. Build your church on the rock of the scriptures.

- The unity of direction and goals among the incoming and established leaders. Do you all want the same thing? Almost every leader says they want to reach their world with the gospel. A stagnant church that is not moving can say what they want, but when a church starts to move, it will determine if they will go there.

- The integrity of the leaders. Anyone can be honest, polite, and peaceful when not challenged. Do the church leaders stand in their integrity when challenged, or do they resort to politics, slander, false accusations, and other alternative methods to achieve their ends?

- Does the Gospel matter? In some church's minds, the church name and its institution are the motivational forces to work to grow the church and not the gospel. When the church is focused on itself and not the Kingdom of God, the other matters of the Kingdom of God will not matter either. Again, these are the fruits of building tribes, not churches.

- In a later chapter, we will look at ministry semantics in that our church cultures are often being defined by definitions and words that do not always mean what you think they mean. I believe you would be surprised by how terms have come to be understood over the lifespan of the church and may answer several questions as to why you feel that you and some in the church are not able to come to a common ground. Definitions of terms and cultures may come from tradition, poor teaching, or preference. You must be working with a shared set of definitions to understand what each side means by what they say. The whole point, for now, is the definition of a culture you are trying to redefine to be more biblical may be clashing with the biblical model though you are using the same terms.

What is a healthy church culture?

A healthy church culture begins with healthy leadership (not just in position but also by influence). Humbly seeking the will of God in His scriptures and operating in our relationships by what we are instructed in the scriptures, seeking peace and reconciliation and not political power. When Titus was to "set in order the things that

is like mine, they were good people, but the authority structure wasn't constitutional or biblical.

An important note is that if the culture inside the church is unhealthy, you will not be able to reach outside the church. When I was a church planter, I spent a lot of my time and energy reaching out to people in evangelism, preaching and ministering to others, etc. When we joined with the other church (and after a honeymoon period), I found myself busy putting out fires and keeping a few unhappy people happy—making multiple trips to people's houses trying to keep them from "leaving the church" and trying to smooth the waters. When you are in a culture that has a lot of controversies, where people who are quick to accuse and get mad and are slow if ever ready to reconcile, you will never be able to move forward because you will be stuck in a swamp of controversy and new people will run. Therefore, culture is the most important thing to change in a church.

The truth is you cannot change the culture overnight. This will be difficult in a culture where situations have been handled poorly for so long and are unhealthy. But the best and quickest way to change a culture is to operate according to healthy practices relationally, ministerially, and culturally. Though you will receive backlash by the unhealthy culture, you will show that the church's new culture is different, biblical, and healthy and will not succumb to these practices nor be bullied into surrender. This will be the foundation by which your church will be able to rebuild itself, better yet, rebuilt by God to shine a light to that community and not taint the reputation of Christ.

The secret of changing culture in the church is not "confronting" the old culture. That is a good way to be removed as the pastor. Remember what I said in an earlier chapter, that a servant of the Lord is to not strive with the contentious but pursue righteousness, faith, love, peace, with them that call on the Lord out of a pure heart. The secret is to live out and example the new culture to the church, build healthy relationships with your people, and plant a new culture in the midst of the old one. People will naturally gravitate toward the healthier culture, and you aim to invest into and grow that new culture. Eventually, the old culture will need to decide if they will join the new, and most will join the new.

CHAPTER FIVE

Starting On the Right Foot

I want to discuss some things that I learned while navigating
uncharted territory. This is the first of 3 parts, the first being
starting on the right foot, the second is dealing with church
problems as they come, and the third is about breaking the curse.
One of the most valuable tools you can have is understanding some
of the strong personalities you will face in ministry. Most people are
great and easily get along but, there will be strong personalities that
will fragrance your church. This is not an exhaustive list and is best
to be joined with other books regarding personalities in the church.

People pt. 1 strong personalities

In ministry, you will face a broad range of strong personalities. It
is good to understand different personalities and understand your
natural personality traits. People are not this cut and dry and will
have a blend of these and other characteristics just like you do, and
this list is not exhaustive, but I want to point out some of the strong
personalities you will possibly meet along the way.

The struggle with a small church in dire need of revitalization
and has been in a rut of "struggling" is that they create the perfect

situation for problems to come in, perhaps even a breeding ground for abuses. They are often short-staffed with few volunteers; they are living in the shadow of a former life that they want to get back to, thus creating a vacuum of need that the church desires to fill. Because of the low numbers rather in the budget, people, or resources, the church has few options on filling the church's vacuum. Because of this, sometimes these vacuums are filled with great people (let me say that first) but who often would not function well in a healthy situation. But because the church needs people, they will install people that may be gifted in their areas but not relationally healthy. This is where many problems make their way into leadership or influence in the church.

The users and abusers

The truth is we are all users to a point. Even our most selfless actions often have some benefit towards our wellbeing. Indeed, the only real "non-user" was Christ, who gave it all to save an undeserving people. However, some users are more prominent in ministry, and their actions are a bit more obvious and perhaps striking. I believe this mentality can cause a lot of contention in the church and often leads to unhealthy and sometimes abusive behavior. When someone is a user to an unhealthy extreme, they feed a personal need in their life and use people, churches, and relationships to feed their needs.

Fortunately, there are some common characteristics that we can observe that will give us a basic understanding of how and why they do what they do. First off, you need to understand that these people cause such problems because they view people, relationships, and churches as a means to feed a personal need. When those things do not feed that need, contention or drama often breaks out to bring the situation back. A user can manifest with many different characteristics, but the common ones are:

- There is an underlying "need" that comes with a condition for their participation.
- They may have a history of "jumping ship" when their conditions are not met.
- They rarely resolve problems since the other person is not as vital as filling their relationship needs.
- They form and break relationships based on how well that relationship feeds their need.
- They join and serve in ministries that provide avenues to meet their need.
- They dispose of relationships that no longer "feed their need."

What are some of these needs?

- Control/Authority- Some people must have "their" way. They are happy and supportive as long as they have their way, but as soon as another decision is made, look out!
- Position- Some people must be top dogs and cannot submit to the authority of other leaders. The best leader is also the best follower.
- Attention- When someone must be on center stage and given accolades
- Comparison- When someone must be viewed as better than others
- Conformity- When someone polices the church to make it exactly as they want, often demanding submission to their point of view.
- Pity- Some people live on the pity of others.
- Familiarity- People hate change.
- Security- Some people find security in the way things are.

What fuels these needs?

- Ego/Pride- These fuel control, authority, position, comparison, conformity, and even pity. As long as someone is willing to fill their need by stroking a person's ego or pride in the way the user deems appropriate, all things will remain stable; but when a person no longer "fills that need," the user will react.
- Idolatry- As Christians, our security is in Christ. Still, when we place our identity in a building, name, songs, services, pews, etc., and they become more important than Christ, the gospel, and even the people of the church, they become idols.
- Security- People can be insecure. This causes them to look for security in other things, which will drive them to mistreat power, people, and principles as those listed above to feel secure.

When they decide to dispose of a relationship

This comes when a user decides to dispose of relationships; they often do not just leave but will leave and do one of three things

- Play games- Often, a user who desires to bring relationships back into a using state will play games. They try to create situations that attempt to bring the person(s) back into use. This is done through jealousy, false claims, using other people, and other things to coerce the person back into the using relationship. These people will not be forthright with you because you do not matter, only what you do for them.
- Punish- When a person or church does not feed the need, this person will punish them by causing turmoil.

These people are often miserable and aren't happy until others are miserable with them. That is why they use others to feed "their" need. Sometimes this comes as false accusations, and anything they feel will hurt the person or church that didn't submit to their need. If they can't get what they want, they will try and hurt the church and punish the people.

- Rub it in- when a user finds a new using relationship, they will go out of their way to rub it in the old using relationship's face. It is a way of justifying their behavior and showing the old relationships how replaceable they were.

I have had to sit with several people that didn't understand how or why someone would cause the problems they did, abandon the church and rub it in their faces. The church and its people were used for selfish ends, and the person did not love the church but how the church filled their need. Unfortunately, many of the abuses that happen on more smaller scales in marriages and other relationships also occur in churches. Here are a few personalities that could be classified as users and abusers.

- **The Miserable Martyr**

They are not a martyr, but they consider themselves to be. They feed on the pity and empathy of others, using their "martyrdom" as means to garner attention and sympathy. They tend to exaggerate their giving and sacrifice while diminishing others' giving and sacrifice. They are convinced that they give more, serve more, and sacrifice more than anyone else. They will tell you how they were unappreciated for their sacrifice. They are silent to those they struggle with because fixing the problem (if there is one) is not their aim, but they are vocal to others about their martyrdom because pity is their aim.

- ## The Non-Conformist

This person tries to "challenge the system." The difficulty with this personality is their adamant pursuit of non-conformity to the environment and leaders in the church but the demand that the environment "conform" to them with an alpha complex. They will challenge in one way or another scriptural teaching. They may do something to challenge the preacher or teaching of the church to show their refusal to submit to scripture. They demand conformity from the church to their value system and will sometimes take extreme measures to push that agenda. They aim to "break free" of Christianity by the book, sometimes blaming it as the cause of much injustice. This person will police the church, making an issue out of anything they don't find to be "correct."

- ## The Vocal Victim

"Injustice! Injustice!" This person is similar to the martyr but with a different need to fill. Where the martyr looks for pity and attention, this person looks for an opportunity to justify poor choices/ behavior. They will tell you how they have been mistreated and use it to make poor choices and why you should accept things you usually wouldn't. This person is unstable, and to disagree or try to offer correction results in more of "Injustice! Injustice!" This person is not approachable since everything they disagree with; they use to feed their victimhood. You may feel sympathetic initially, but you will find out that the common denominator of many of their injustices is them.

- ## The Powermonger

Some people need power. They feed an ego that is only filled when they are in authority. When what they say goes. Like many of these characters, they use these traits to feed their need; often, their need is power. Power corrupts if put into the wrong person's hands who cannot identify and control their personality traits. Team leadership is crucial in the church because you give voice to a group of people instead of one person calling the shots. Many of these personalities cannot function in a team environment where everyone is looking to the church as the primary beneficiary because they see the church as an avenue for their benefit.

- **The Machiavelli**

This one makes me sick to my stomach. In a church with multiple ages, a desirable trait is cooperation. This person is not looking to cooperate, tolerate or bend for the rest of the church. They have an end in mind and choose to manipulate conversations, accusations, people, or even pastors to achieve their ends. This person may try to convince you of something that you find extreme or risky, and if you go along to get along, they will use your words and actions against you. They may try to flatter you to get you to agree to things they can use later against you, and if you give an inch, they will leverage you. They may try to get you to remove another leader that they don't like, then they can use that removal as a tool to leverage or remove you. They may ask you to handle money, then accuse you of being too comfortable with money or doing something with it. They are comfortable twisting conversations, making accusations, and even lying to achieve their end because they believe the end justifies the means.

The advice that I will give you for this person is to stick with biblical principles and keep healthy boundaries. If someone tries to get you to agree to something extreme or do something against your convictions, it is best to have a team of leaders or at least witnesses to deal with such situations. These people can't function with witnesses because they will have to answer for their words or actions. The best way to end manipulation is to create transparency.

- **The Bully**

This insecure individual feels like they need to be on top to bolster their security or ego. They will often use tactics of intimidation to coerce the pastor into submission. These tactics of intimidation often come as accusations, threats, or ultimatums. These are not healthy leaders, and though they have a way of making it into leadership, they often will leave if they feel they cannot intimidate the other leaders.

- **The Criticizer**

This is someone who seems like they are never happy. No matter what, they are upset about something and regularly criticize the church or pastor, both privately and publicly. Be patient, and be satisfied that they are honest about their criticisms. Usually, they are not as "unhappy" with you as they appear since their personality contains no filter for complaints.

- **The Politician**

One of the biggest struggles I have had in ministry is the political atmosphere. I have seen some of the same problems in religious politics as in public politics. You will meet great politicians saying the right things at the right time and know how to navigate the political atmosphere. Though diplomacy should be taken, political correctness is alive and well in the church. When encountering this personality and seeing that the person is playing politics and not being honest about the situation, choose to keep some space. You have a job to do, and politics waste your time and energy.

• The Constitutional Priest

Often, it isn't the constitution that will cause you problems; it will be those who feel they can choose the parts that are enforced and those that can be overlooked or redefined. They set themselves as the sole interpreter of the constitution, the sole definer of its terms, and even push that the constitution says something that it doesn't say. They will use the constitutional obliviousness of people in the church to their advantage. The difficulty with this is that the church is not truly operated by the constitution but by the one who stands over it. You will run into hidden rules and find yourself in a maze that you do not know how to navigate, making these person(s) priests of the constitution. You will be expected to comply with their interpretations, definitions, and imaginations. The constitution is supposed to be an objective source of administrative authority by which the institution operates, but it gets turned into a subjective source of contention by those who believe they stand over it.

People pt. 2 families

Hopefully, as your church grows, you reach all ages but especially families (because they are all ages.) What do families feel when they show up? Do they feel like they have walked into a museum where everything is don't touch, don't move, be quiet. Museums are wonderful places, but the church is not a museum. If a church functions as a museum, then all it will be is a memorial. How does your church handle toys on the lawn, crumbs on the floor, and an occasional spill of a drink? How would they like for kids to be involved in the services? My kids come up to me all the time during church; I don't dismiss them. Just because I am at church doesn't mean that I am not a dad. My wife has led singing with a baby in her arms. The church is a family first, not an institution with rituals. If a church emphasizes a building with ceremonies and memorials, that is what it will have, and that is what it will be, but if a church emphasizes the power of the gospel in the lives of people, that is what it will have, and that is what it will be. We do not emphasize the building or rituals, or memorials. We emphasize the gospel in the lives of people and their families. The building is just a tool, and our practices must be purposeful and biblical, not just traditional.

I was concerned because I wanted families to be welcome at our church, including kids. I noticed like some houses where you can't touch anything or play because everything had to be so so, so was our church. I have four kids, and I felt embarrassed that my kids got toys out or left crumbs on the floor, and if I felt this way, so would other families. We worked on the kids to clean up their messes and developed systems to ensure the building was clean, but if families feel embarrassed or put down for their kids, you will lose them. The building is a tool to reach people with the gospel. The church building is often treated as a classic car, pristine and beautiful but only used on special occasions when it needs to be treated like a minivan, a vehicle to bring the people inside to their destination. The classic car is beautiful when the minivan is functional; the classic car is an idol, and the minivan, a tool.

People pt. 3 relationships

As you navigate the territory, you will encounter relationship practices that aren't healthy. As you have already read, unhealthy relationships lead to unhealthy churches. Whether you are talking about friendships, marriages, or churches, harmful relationship practices lead to unhealthy relationships. Many relationships go sour, not because of the other individual but how we handle the other individual. If a relationship is full of games, gossip, and other relationship-destroying habits, you will have to deal with it. Again, you will find that others who do not choose a healthy resolution process with people will do the same to you.

You have zero control of the actions and words of others, but you need to stay in complete control of your actions and words. Reacting poorly to poorly acting people only makes problems more prominent. There is no excuse to stoop to the levels of those who have chosen to oppose you. Keep your integrity, be honest, and do not get sucked into the games. Eventually, people will notice the difference between your healthy response and their non-healthy response. Unhealthy people will realize you will not play their games and will either adopt healthier practices or leave. At times, when I felt tempted to respond poorly, I repeated to myself over and over: "Act, do not react." The first healthy relationship starts with you, not them. Handle things biblically, and honestly and honest people will see it.

People pt.4 criticism

One of the most significant reasons revitalization efforts fail is the barrage of criticism launched against the new pastor and his family. Criticism can cripple revitalization efforts either because the pastor cannot handle all the criticism from people on social media or in the church, or it creates a hostile environment against any meaningful growth. You need to know that criticism is unavoidable, you can be a great diplomat, but there will always be those who act like sports critics; you won't see them on the field, but they will tell you all the mistakes you made while on it. Here is a process to know if the criticism is worth the time of day.

How to handle criticism, take the test:

- Is the criticism true or factual, or is it just emotion?
  - If true, how can you correct it?
  - How can you keep from making the same mistake again?
  - If emotional, please move to the next step.

- What is the motive of the criticizer?
  - o Is the criticizer open to being corrected?
  - o Are there demands behind the criticism that are unreasonable?
  - o Does a threat accompany the criticism?
  - o Is there an agenda that they want to achieve?
- Is the criticism in line with the scriptures?
  - o What is the verse?
  - o How can we be more biblical?

We all make mistakes, I have been rebuked many times by many people, but I have learned to heed criticisms of those based on scripture and those based on reality. You cannot answer criticisms outside of that box, and I would encourage you to take the test and see if it is something to lose sleep over.

Understand present semantics

When you speak to your church, there is often a significant difference between what you said and what they heard, especially with people looking for ways to be offended. In the beginning, they may give you some grace, but in situations of contention, they will most likely assume the worst and apply their perceptions accordingly. I figured out very quickly that I never said anything that didn't have political ramifications. If a person or a group is suspicious of you and looking for evidence to support their suspicions, you don't have to say something offensive for them to be upset or declare you guilty.

The problem with this is they apply meaning to your words. If they are honest with you about this, you will be able to correct the meaning of your words so they can understand what you meant by what you said. But if they are already convinced, you may never be able to convince them otherwise. The other difficulty with this type of behavior is that you will always be "explaining" your innocence to their perceptions. They will wear you out if they are unwilling to love you by thinking the best instead of assuming the worst.

Now that you have some tools to get you started on the right foot, let's move into navigating challenges that you will face on this journey of revitalization.

Chapter Six

Taking on the Challenges

─────

As you navigate uncharted territory, you will have to deal with problems. A member of my church told me that they were told that our church was cursed, which is why it had these problems all these years. In churches where contention is more of a norm, you will need to face these problems not just to keep them at bay but eventually solve them. The practice of overlooking issues and turning a blind eye to issues in the church is *NOT* the solution. The same issues in the secular world also occur in the church world. But there is hope in solving some of the problems you encounter in your effort to break the curse of contention at the church.

Start by doing the right things

Don't begin by confronting the wrong things; start by doing the right things. The best cure for the disease of contention is strengthening the church's immune system. If you want to successfully bring this church out of contention, start by strengthening the church body because it will be this body that will either defeat the cancer of contention within it or succumb to it. Start with a healthy diet of the scriptures in the church's regular activities, using the bible not only from the pulpit but in every meeting you go to. Remember, the bible is the book of the church, and you as the spiritual leader need to keep that book in front of the people, open and applied. Add a few spiritual vitamins of spiritually strong people and invest into the body to give it the tools necessary to defeat the disease and build itself up. The best medicine is not railing against disease but strengthening the body to heal itself and overcome the disease.

If you walk into these churches and start confronting people and "putting them straight," you will lose the church. Again, you must give the church a clean slate. Part of my advice to our leaders as they worked with problems was to inform the individual of the problem and provide them with a chance to do it right. They can't fix something they do not know is an issue. I always wanted to give people opportunities to do it right and only confronted them when I felt there was no other solution. With that said, start doing the right things in the church, act and work as if the church is healthy, and do the right things, and as time goes on, people will gravitate to the healthier practices as you are setting the pace for the new culture.

If you have deacons, work with them as deacons assuming the best, that they are there to exercise their calling as deacons to minister to the church. Find ways they can start ministering to the church according to the bible and the constitution. If you have other leaders, work within the constitution's constraints and become familiar with the working relationships the constitution grants and take problems and contentions as they come, and they will come. You can't fix everything all at once; you take this one bite at a time. Let's look at what you can expect and how you can remedy the problem.

The leadership in the church

Church revitalization of contentious churches will have some unique challenges that I want to touch on. You are asked as a revitalizing pastor to turn an institution around, meaning you must deal with the things that brought that institution to this point in its lifecycle. It's going to take honesty, a focus on reality, and some intentional decisions. You can't just fire the people causing the problems as in the business world, but if you focus on building the church's health, especially in the leadership, healthy leaders will come and stay, and unhealthy leaders will be made to choose to grow or go.

The first problem that you must solve is not creating one. I cannot say that all my decisions were spot on, but I learned early on that there is safety in the multitude of counselors.[15] Men more competent than me and godlier than me are treasure troves of knowledge and wisdom that often go untapped. Make your decisions, handle your relationships and live your life with scripture in the center. Have people around you that exhort you according to the scriptures and keep you accountable both inside your church and outside your church; these perspectives will be vital as you navigate problems that are killing the church.

One mistake I see a lot of churches make that creates problems is they give into the leadership vacuum. The institutional part of the church leads them to want to fill positions they feel they must have, and they fill these positions based on a supposed need instead of the presence of a qualified candidate. They will install leaders, deacons, elders, ministers, pastors, etc., because they feel if they do not have them, they are missing something, and they end up installing people that either are not gifted, called, or qualified in those ministries.

It is better not to have a position in the church than to have a person not qualified in that position. Don't give in to the leadership vacuum. If you feel like God wants you to have a particular position, pray to God to bring people in that will fulfill these ministries according to the bible or that someone in your flock will become evident. If you don't have anyone, then maybe God doesn't want

---

[15] Proverbs 11:14

that position in the church right now. Work with what God has given you, and stop trying to fill the shoes of other institutions. If you are looking for a position that you feel needs filled, write down precisely what you think the Lord wants and fill that position but just not with anybody; as the spiritual leader, your aim is to lead your congregation to install people of a qualified caliber.

The leadership vacuum is caused by a few things: the first being tradition; if a church traditionally has four deacons, but there are no men that want to be a deacon or meet the biblical qualifications, it is not wise to install anyone to that position, secondly, by the pressure from others. Just because someone is a nice person and is well-liked doesn't mean they will function well in all positions. Thirdly, impatience. I know the excitement of a growing church, and I understand the excitement of filling positions, but not everyone was a good fit, and they left a hole that I created. Lastly, understand that strong personalities will most likely make it into positions when these vacuums exist. Sometimes, they will not necessarily qualify biblically for the positions, but they make it because of their personality.

You will not choose who you will have to work with but work with whom you are given. There are avenues to invest in people to help develop them into healthy leaders or servants, and you should take advantage of those resources. As problems arise, handle them like you would if your church was healthy. You need to initiate a healthier culture by dealing with issues in healthy ways. Give people a chance to do it right, but do not sweep problems under the rug.

What do you do with leaders you already have? You inherited these leaders, you are not sure you would have installed them, but you have them. Again, start at a place of health, talk with them about their ministries and aid them in developing themselves and their ministries. Act as if they are healthy leaders working in their ministries. Most of the people will be great, and if you take the time to get to know them and help them, you will find their heart for the ministry is a lot like yours. But what do you do with leaders who are not fulfilling their ministries?

One of the characteristics of a contentious dying church is they have positions but little fulfillment. Unfortunately, what happens in these churches is people use their position as an avenue to control the other parts of the ministry. The ministry that their position entails is all but non-existent as they use their title to show up to leadership and control the church. Exhortations to bring their ministry up to speed will fall on deaf ears because they have redefined their role. Their time is not spent fulfilling their ministry but watching the other ministries and the pastor, often being a source of contention.

Again, it is not wise to remove them because of the political fallout and the removal of the opportunity to bring them back into healthy ministry. Remember Paul's exhortation to Timothy to focus his attention on healthy Christian attributes with those who are also calling on the Lord out of a pure heart while giving the opposition a chance for God to work in their hearts. If you focus on the contentious, that will spell disaster. Keep encouraging them to fulfill their ministry and ask how their ministry is going. Keep them in the loop with the other leaders so they are surrounded by people who are participating in the life of the church so that they have a ship to board. Give them many chances to do it right. If they refuse to get on board, the gulf between them and the rest of the leadership will be evident to you and the other leaders.

Deep-rooted problems

If you buy a piece of property that needs fixing up, you will find that there are small things that need to be done, but you will also find things that have been let go for so long that they have become huge problems, deeply rooted, and sometimes can only be fixed by tearing the whole thing out. In ministry, you are inheriting a few things, with the blessing of the people and the church to which you are called; you will also find problems that have been let go for so long that they have become deeply rooted and extremely difficult to deal with.

The problem with quick turnover rates of pastors is that they do not stay long enough to work through specific issues and the problems become worse. Not only that but you are asked to work with the circumstances given you by previous pastors and leaders in the church. You will have no idea what some of these are until you are in it. I found things and people refreshing and wonderful when coming into this church. But there were several things that I would never have done, nor would I have been comfortable at a church with these kinds of decisions. You must determine in your heart how to work the church through these difficulties and problems, which some have become deeply rooted.

You've read about unhealthy relationship practices; you've read about installing people into positions they shouldn't be in. You need to know that certain sins in the church are blasted and certain sins in the church are permissible as understood by a tribe mentality. Church discipline has disappeared from the church because our values dictate tradition, institutionalism, peace at all costs, political correctness, numbers, money, tribal preservation, etc. A form of tribalism has either been adopted over the years or has been there from the onset. For many, the process of discipline or the confronting of sin is met with hostility because these are considered sins against the tribe. Understand that a true church is not a tribe but a community who have cast their allegiance to Jesus, are submissive to God's Word, and put purity to God as the context of unity. As the new pastor, you must exercise your ministry according to the bible and possibly discipline behavior that has tainted the church for many years. This is extremely hard for both the pastor and the people as these deeply rooted sins get worked out and are another cause for the failure of revitalization efforts. Better to fail doing the right thing than to succeed by doing the wrong thing.

Unseen challenges

The difficulty is that these churches often run at high risk, either financially, legally, or ministerially as seen in chapter one. These churches will often have little to no policies in protecting children, how to handle sex offenders, facility use policies, homosexual marriage, etc. Many churches have never had to worry about many of the current problems today's churches face. If they are unwilling to come up to the times, by taking on this church the pastor could be putting himself and his people at tremendous risk.

We live in a day where lawsuits are a reality for the church, and if the church does not have a clear constitution and policies to protect the church and its people, it could spell legal/moral or financial disaster. The constitution should make you comfortable for you and your people to serve under. The constitution can be lengthy, complicated, and even contradicting in these churches because they are old and often amended to consolidate control. This is not a good situation and should be remedied as soon as ministerially possible. Start by putting administrative policies in place to protect the church under more ordinary circumstances, like with children or facility use.

Again, these churches that have not taken these things seriously will be offended that they must undergo procedures. Sometimes they won't understand the church's risk by not having them. I know for me, we had put in place a facility use request for non-members, and sure enough, I became a social media thread for such an "insulting request" to use the facility even after trying to explain why these policies mattered. These churches will run at high risk because they do not understand the need for policies and procedures to protect the church and those who serve in it. Many don't understand the current culture and have little exposure to current legal difficulties. I found out after I was hired that our church was at tremendous financial, legal, and insurability risk. I can't go into detail, but I almost walked out after learning about these risks.

It is problems like these that are unseen that you will have to deal with. You need to make sure you and your people are protected. Don't play games in these circumstances. In any other career field, companies offer protection for their employees; the same should be for those serving in the ministry. The stories of pastors who had to endure ministerial ruin are often buried. I have met pastors and former pastors that put themselves at risk and paid for it. Please be careful who you entrust yourself, your members, and your family to. With that, there are ways to break the curse, which is the next chapter's topic.

Chapter Seven

Breaking the Curse

L ike I told you before, almost two years into this process, one of my members who had been at the church for many years informed me that they were told that the church was cursed and has suffered all these years under that curse. Later, a former member confirmed this who left a little over ten years before my arrival. If your church is cursed with contention, then I want to give you the avenues by which will help you break it, not only for the church but hopefully for the contentious to have more healthy relationships with the body of believers.

Now, I am not sure if the church was cursed, but I suddenly knew that God wanted to break this cycle of turnover and hostility that had plagued the church for many years. In dying churches with contention, the cycle that often plagues them must be stopped. A pastor must stay long enough and bear through the difficulties to bring the church to the other side. Pastors that just leave because of difficulty haven't helped the church. If you look in the book of Titus at the job of the elders and overseers, it was primarily to bring the church to order and deal with the problems that put the church out of order. Titus was to "set in order the things that are lacking." That is the call of the revitalizer of a contentious church. Every church is different, but some things can help you "break the curse."

Invest in the healthy culture

In Chapter 4, I discussed the idea of planting a healthy culture in the church. I want to reiterate that. The worst thing a pastor could do is isolate himself from other leaders and the people. In a church, you need to spend your time investing in a healthy culture. Breaking the curse is not an easy feat, and attempting to do so prematurely will result in failure. There need to be several things in place when the curse comes to haunt you. It would help if you were strategic because your time is critical; you do not know the timeline you have to work with. In churches where contention is making itself more and more comfortable, they will have less tolerance and patience and react more and more quickly with each passing instance. Like a bad habit that starts with just a little, it will become worse and more frequent if it is not brought into subjection. These relational bad habits will become more frequent as the person(s) becomes more tolerant with them in their lives. So, when you are adjusting your time, I would follow this pattern:

1. Spend most of your time with your leaders. I would say that this should take up most of your relationship time. You only have so much time, and the best thing you could do for your people is have growing relationships with those who serve your people.

2. Spend more of your time building those relationships with your people. Ultimately, we grew enough to hit critical mass early on by those who were part of the new culture and those coming into the new culture. It is not that you don't want to spend time with people outside of your church, but God put you in that church for those people, and they need to be your focus.

3. Spend some time getting to know new people. As your church grows, your relationships with possible leaders and members will be vital to developing a healthy base for your

church to stand and grow. With each phase of growth, your base will need to be stronger.

The decision-making process

Do not to make hasty decisions. You would be surprised how a good night's sleep and some space will clear your head about the pressures you feel at the church. There will always be people and situations that will pressure you to decide quickly or to get you to promise something. Don't cave in at the moment; you can always call another meeting. Some people use the tactics of car salespeople. That is to get you to decide now before you have time to go home and think about it. Most car sales are made on the spot by the convincing or pressuring of a good salesperson. I created a 24-hour window to help me avoid making a hasty decision in the moment of pressure. This is good for decisions and for dealing with threats.

Wisdom understands that people are emotional, including you. Some allow their emotions to carry more weight than others. Though feelings can be wonderful, they can also be awful in moments of tremendous stress and contention. Understand that emotion is not a stable tool to interpret circumstances or handle them. That is why not you shouldn't allow yourself to get worked up and give yourself some space. You need to understand your emotional tendencies; many pastors have gotten themselves in trouble by reacting poorly to poorly acting people.

The decision to stay

Don't give up too quickly; one month can change so much. Deciding too soon in the heat of the moment is a mistake. If God is shutting that door that quickly, they will fire you but don't just quit. When we went through the most challenging portion of this process, I thought everyone had enough of me. Later in pastor appreciation month, I came to find out that the congregation appreciated that I stood on God's Word in the face of adversity. You don't know what is going on behind the scenes. Stay as long as God has you there, don't quit just because it gets hard. No one did anything significant for God easily.

Keep your face in the scriptures. You would be surprised at the values and priorities other people and ministers put on you. Your goal is to operate your ministry according to the scriptures and not the changing winds of church politics. You need to humble yourself before the scriptures and allow them to be the authority by which you operate your ministry, not your emotion, politics, or bullies. This goes for standing for the right things despite tremendous opposition and admitting where you fell short. I know for me, I went and repented to a brother that I wronged because though I was trying to make a good decision, the scriptures showed me where I was wrong. You are not perfect, don't pretend to be.

When contention comes and you are attacked

In the heat of the attack, it is easy to justify you defending yourself or to condemn your attackers, but scripture tells us not to avenge ourselves[16] and that the servant of the Lord must not quarrel but be gentle.[17] You have a purpose there; they are not attacking you; they are attacking the One who sent you. I promise you, if you fight back, you will lose the church. All your doing is giving them more ammunition to use against you, and it's probably a trap. You stick to the bible, make good decisions, continue to act in a way that brings honor to God.

They may not be persecuting you because of the name of Jesus, but they are persecuting you because of the Word of Jesus.

---

[16] Romans 12:17-21
[17] 2 Timothy 2:24-26

In these moments, the congregation is watching the actions of the leaders of the church. The church will judge the leaders based on their actions. They will not see or feel the pressure put on you by the contentious; all they will see is your reaction. Pastors who choose to react will not aid their cause in the face of contention. The best avenue is to continue to *pursue righteousness, faith, love, and peace, with those who call on the Lord out of a pure heart.*[18] Don't be afraid to answer questions and be willing to be transparent. Show your congregation you have nothing to hide and are eager to continue to serve even in the face of opposition. This will not be characteristic of the contentious because they will need to control the information to win people over. Meet with the contentious but only with witnesses, as you will read later in this book. All the times that I have become defensive and tried to justify myself never accomplished its purpose; it only made things worse in the world of church politics. Learn from me; it's not worth it.

An approach to stabilizing your family

In breaking the curse, many tactics are used to end a revitalization process. Bi-vocational ministry is a ready solution to some of these. In my work as a church planter and church revitalizer, I have first-hand experience of the benefits of bi-vocational ministry. Though it comes with its own unique set of challenges, it also comes with many perks. One of the most significant reasons is money; before they throttled up the political machine, I was given an ultimatum to cease what I was doing, or I would lose the church; which frightened my family, but we knew that we had another income we could depend on and this person couldn't touch that income. There is something healthy about the fact that one person couldn't control me by threatening my family's well-being, especially if that

[18] 2 Timothy 2:22b MEV

person is unstable. It was also good for the church that we just cut our budget to meet the new giving, and though we had to make some significant cuts, they could not bankrupt the church.

Bi-vocational ministry has many advantages for your family and your finances, security, and health. It is also a blessing to a church struggling to make it. There are more advantages than I have room to mention, but I would recommend pastors work outside the church to revitalize that church. Being strategic about your secular job can not only provide financial security for your family but also create avenues of connections into the community, earning respect for being a working pastor, a higher tolerance for family time, and more reasonable expectations from your church.

The key to breaking the curse

The Key to breaking the Curse is building a team of mighty men. We read in the conquests of David, his leadership quality was secure enough to have strong men around him and, in many cases, were probably more competent than him. David was strong not because he was personally strong but was given favor by the Lord and was surrounded by strong men that followed him. The Lord made David greater and greater, and He did so by bringing into his life mighty men that shouldered the will of God for David with him. This is what 1 Chronicles 11:7-11a says

> *Then David dwelt in the stronghold; therefore, they called it the City of David. And he built the city around it, from the Millo to the surrounding area. Joab repaired the rest of the city. So David went on and became great, and the Lord of hosts was with him. Now these were the heads of the mighty men whom David had, who strengthened themselves with him in his kingdom, with*

> all Israel, to make him king, according to the word of the
> Lord concerning Israel.[19]

If God wants to revitalize this contentious church, you will need to be strong and courageous. You will have to be surrounded by people who will strengthen themselves with you to take on the challenges that you will face. These are the people who will stand with you as you shoulder the burden of the political war. In the past, when pastors failed to revitalize the church I was in, they did not have strong leaders around them and thus shouldered the burden alone.

Scripturally, men are to take the leadership role, so finding men who are mighty enough to stand, humble enough to cooperate, wise enough to act with tact, and godly enough to act with integrity will be crucial. Though I do not want to diminish the strong godly women God used as they continued to show up, stand up and serve even amid this war waged against the church. It took the strength of all of them to carry this church forward. My part was very little compared to the power of my people. How do you know that the tension is rising in your church? Let's look at that next.

---

[19] NKJV

CHAPTER EIGHT

Signs of Rising Tensions

———

Assuming you are moving the church forward, people are being reached, and the church is growing, there are a few things to look out for. This is one of the reasons that I am not an advocate to change the church until you have changed the church's culture. Because if the culture of your church hasn't changed, your efforts at changing the church will be in vain and will end up in disaster. You should be preaching the vision and core values as you redirect the church culture into a healthier direction. As I prayed, I felt the Lord wanted me to preach the vision of the church and emphasize the core values that Christ and the apostles gave the church. So that is what I did. I embarked on communicating and convincing the church to see herself in the light of her Creator, that she was brought together for a purpose by God, that she had as her guide God's Word and that the blood of Christ purchased her for Christ and that she was His church, to operate under His headship through His Word.

Like I said before, one of the hardest things to do is change a culture. Timelines to do this are entirely dependent on several factors like the church's financial stability, the openness of the people to change, the rate of growth that takes place, the willingness of the pastor to endure the old culture, etc. This timeline can be anywhere from a year or two to five to ten years or possibly longer. We knew that it would take time and God's favor to change this culture. One thing that separates our story from others is that I changed little to nothing in the church outside the church's name. My goal wasn't for a young church; my goal was for a biblical church, a multigenerational church. I wanted my kids to see godly people of all ages working together, ministering to one another, and loving each other as the church lives out the gospel as a light for the community.

As you move forward in this path, you will begin to notice resistance to this movement by the old culture. Not everyone in the old culture will resist (some will be praising Jesus for seeing the church finally move forward). But the deeper part of the old culture that made it what it was will start to resist the new culture. There are various reasons; everything from tradition to control will fuel the tension between old and new cultures. This is an excellent time to see the tribes that make up your church. This old tribe will not join the new culture because the new is "different." A few things are indicators of this rising tension that I want to point out for you.

Jesus said to the Pharisees, *"O you hypocrites, you can discern the face of the sky, but you cannot discern the signs of the times."*[20] No one will come and tell you that the tension is rising in your church. You will be surprised how in the dark you are until the day comes when "it" happens. A typical transition will take place in your church as it grows. If your deeper parts of the original church members are not really in favor of moving forward, you will see the "them and us" mentality transition into the "them or us" mentality. They are starting to reject the new culture and the new people that come with it. There are a few indicators that will help you notice this pattern. Here is a pattern of many revitalization efforts with descriptions. The rest of the chapter will provide more detail of the signs of this process in the church.

---

[20] Matthew 16:3 MEV

- **Us and You:** The church will have an initial excitement for the prospect of a new pastor. Every church will see an influx of new people who want to hear him preach, meet him and his family, and get to know what kind of pastor he will be. This is commonly called the honeymoon period. The church has no experience with the pastor, either good or bad, and is excited about the potential of growth and even possibly saving their church.

- **Us and Them:** With the new pastor, if he is doing his part to reach out to his community with the aid of the excited church, the numbers will increase. This increase will come by word of mouth, relationships with the community, and the faithful sharing of the gospel. The church will be excited about the growth, the new people, the Sunday school rooms that are starting to fill up, and the pews they once saw empty will have new faces in them.

- **Us or Them:** People will start joining the church, and the church will begin showing signs of new life as new people start filling in positions of the church. This will become uncomfortable with some who now must share leadership with these new people. They start losing their power over the church as this new culture takes root. This, unfortunately, leads to a toxic response that often stalls the progress of meaningful growth and is the point where the old culture has rejected the new culture with its people, and tensions will start to rise between the two cultures. The old culture will not be satisfied with the new, and the "us and them" will be transitioned into "us or them." At this time, you will see factions start to form, and pressure will be placed on people in the church to "choose a side." If this doesn't work to bring the church back, this will lead to the next step.

- **Us or You:** This will ultimately result in an attempt to coerce the pastor to choose between the two cultures.

The pastor is put in a place where he must either reject the new culture and submit to the old culture or reject the old culture in favor of the new. This is a place that no pastor wants to be in; the goal is for a healthy church where the old and new can worship together, but if the old culture factions themselves off of the new culture and pits themselves against it, they will attempt to make you (and others) decide between the two. If you choose not to remove the new culture, this will result in their target being transferred from the new culture to its leader...you.

One of the most notable signs is the criticism that arises from the old culture of the pastor who is representing the new culture. You, as a pastor, need to minister to the whole church and look for ways to be involved in the different generations and involve the generations together. I always loved ministering to the older generation, to know their life stories and testimonies of how God worked in their lives. However, with new families attending the church, you will need to be available to minister to them as well. We are there to minister to the whole body. The "them or us" mentality will often view this as a betrayal because they believe their time at the church, financial contribution, or other sacrifices garner more emphasis from the pastor. Favoritism is a sin, and you should avoid it. However, to put the pastor in a position where he must choose one part of the body or the other is a sure sign that they are not embracing the new culture.

Another thing to look for is that members of the original culture stop participating in their ministries, especially when working with new people. This may start as simply no longer participating in the ministries, but it will probably turn into resignations over time. To answer why this takes place is different with each person, but I think we can point out some common characteristics of this behavior.

Participation usually suspends when members of the old

culture in those ministries disapprove of how the new team leader (director) exercises the ministry. You would hope that these members would communicate to the new director about their concerns and suggestions on how the ministry has been operated in the past or try to find quick resolutions, but that is not how some will handle it. They will stop participating and wait for the leader to come to them, which by the time the leader figures it out, the person will usually be upset for more than the original problem. The problem with this approach is the leader is kept in a level of suspense of if their committee or team are on board or not, and it turns into a game that no one knows the rules to. Sometimes these people will start to "tattle" on each other instead of talking to each other, making everything a pastor's problem and more significant than it needs to be. Then will come the "unless x, y, and z are fixed, I am not working with that person."

Having people who communicate when they have an issue is vital to quick and painless resolutions, but having people who choose to use ulterior methods to drive their point leads to unnecessary drama and a culture of insecurity and instability. We once had a committee director over a ministry previously run by someone who stepped down from the director position to just being on the committee. The new director was in tears because she had no idea what was happening when the former director just quit showing up and wouldn't respond to the director's efforts to reach out. I called a meeting between them because both parties approached me with their side, and though they were upset at me for calling the meeting to bring everything to the table, they had dealt with their issues and reconciled after a couple of hours. I wish I could say that was the end of the problem, but as long as those practices occur, these issues will rise again and again.

Resignations will start to slowly appear as members begin to reject the church's new direction. Though there may be a few, most will not resign yet. Those who quit you will often find to be upset when their position is given to someone else after their resignation. You may find yourself making multiple trips to people's houses, putting out fires, and trying to convince some people not to resign their positions; this is a true sign that tensions are growing. Why are these things taking place? Because the culture leading to the church's death was now beginning to resist the new direction and people coming into the ministry. Resignations are a way to show their disapproval and stall the process. Some will probably only stay in those positions as long as you pursue them and meet their demands, which will burn you out. Please note that this is a minority of the original people. Not everyone will do this, but there will be a few. I was told, "let's see how you like when you don't have positions a, b and c!"

In line with these, you will begin to see controversies arise that demand your immediate attention and defense. These controversies act like trials; the old culture keeps trying to bring the new culture into trial before them. They will make accusations against the new culture or its people and demand answers and ultimately conformity. You will find yourself regularly giving a defense before the court of the old culture on behalf of the new culture. At the beginning of revitalization, this fits in the parameters of communicating the new vision of the church and is a normal part of the process. Still, as time goes on, there will be those who are not looking to understand the new culture but keep their influence over it. If you are regularly finding yourself being brought before a group of the old culture to answer accusations and perceptions, know the tension is rising. This will lead to the next era of pressure in the church—the Deep Church-State.

CHAPTER NINE

The Deep Church-State
and the Widening Gulf

The next thing you will meet is the deep church-state. In conspiracy theories, there is a theory of the deep state. As I understand it, it is the theory that public offices of the government, like the president, senate, etc., are nothing more than a façade and that the real ruling authorities hide behind this façade and rule the government. Unfortunately, this is not just a theory in many churches. I will give you some advice regarding your relationship with the deep church-state that will save your ministry at the church. There is often a deep ruling church-state hidden in the façade of a congregational constituted church. This state is often only prosperous when operating in the dark when no one can validate what is said or done behind closed doors. The back-door meetings are real and hidden from the body of believers because transparency and information to the rest would expose this state.

As you are working with the people and new people are coming on and having a say with the direction of the church, the ruling sect will expose themselves, and you will find out who really runs the church. This group will probably not meet you with intentions of cooperating but to put you in your place. I wish I could say otherwise, but many of these will use some of the tactics discussed in this chapter to coerce you. This may sound extreme, but the corruption in public politics is mirrored in the religious world in some instances. Some churches have an unwritten rule to run everything through this group before bringing anything before the congregation, regardless of the constitutional process. Again, your conversations with previous pastors will prove vital as you will learn what they went through as they worked with this deep state.

When you meet the deep church-state, you need to turn on the light switch and make everything transparent. This doesn't mean that you go around proclaiming the deep church-state to the church; that is a sure way to get fired. Instead, find ways to create transparency in the church, especially among the leaders. If you are working with integrity, you should have nothing to hide. Endeavor to develop levels of transparency in the leadership that mirror the honesty of the new culture. Here are some ways to bring light to a dark situation.

- An email chain; that way, conversations have a record of you with other leaders and your work among the committees.
- Have an objective party take minutes of all your meetings (like old constitutions told you to do)
- Do not meet with the deep church-state privately; all meetings should be held with other leaders present.
- Keep as much as you can before the congregation.
- Be leery of phone calls, private confrontations, or if a person waits until witnesses leave. If they can't say what they want with witnesses, you do not need to talk to them. (this has happened to me several times)

The other thing you should do is equip and inform your church. In America, we hear that an uninformed voter is a poor voter. This is true, even in the church world. Uninformed church members are taken advantage of. The catholic church tried to keep the bible out of the hands of people, so they could control what people believed. This is not a dead tactic. The control of information is a tool for political leverage. During the situation, I had a pastor friend who I thought would help, who told me that his advice to me and others was never to put anything in writing; that way, they wouldn't have to answer for it. My response is two words: corrupt politics. The integrity of a pastor committed to Jesus will demand honesty and integrity, not slimy games.

How can someone make exhortations about the constitution, the bible, situations, and conversations that aren't true and yet be believed? That is to keep their followers in the dark. They must remain the channel of information for the church, and transparency is their enemy. Education with information is another step in the right direction. Hold meetings with both the leadership and the congregation over the constitution of the church, create transparency on matters that are not confidential and create an open environment. You will find that the work you do in this area now will soften the blow they will have when they decide to throttle up the political machine. Keeping information accessible will allow people the resources to determine if what they are being told is true.

Eventually, a decision will be made either by the congregation or the leaders that the old culture will deem as the breaking point and will be significant enough that they will attempt to reverse the decision. Again, if the decision is reversed, they have pulled the church back into control. This is hard to discuss because every pastor naturally wants everyone to get along, but if you have a growing church that is doing the work, and you have a shrinking sect that is trying to bring the church back underneath them, you have to choose what is the right thing for the church. If you work in a congregational government, then go to the congregation. The church needs to decide as a whole.

The old culture will attempt to bring the church back under their control and will use various means to do so. Depending on where you are in the revitalization process will determine the intensity and success of their endeavor. You will need to note the following avenues sometimes used to control people, pastors, and churches:

- Control by Intimidation- Unfortunately, this exists in churches. In its most basic form, it is a way to show the pastor who is the real boss of the church. Intimidation can be used on the leaders and the congregation and is a form of bullying the church. You overcome this by empowering the congregation to do what is right, not succumb to bullying, and stand firm with your people and God's Word. You make decisions by the principles found in scripture, not the pressure put on you by intimidation. Titus most likely used Paul's letter to him as the authority against abuse in the church, and we have the scriptures for our use.

- Control by accusation- You are guilty till proven innocent. This is a tactic used to keep you on the defensive. Suppose you are regularly having to defend yourself and prove your innocence (or the innocence of the new culture) against accusations. In that case, you will ultimately act according to their whims because you are fearful of their allegations and perceptions. These will burn you out emotionally, take up precious time and keep you from moving forward into a healthy culture. In its most basic form, it will follow the pattern of "I (or others) think you are trying to do x, y, or z. If you don't do a, b or c, then we know you are guilty." Sadly, the only real solution is not giving your time or energy to the accusation. You don't want to exit the world of accountability, but this can be abused, and you need to discern when it is. You cannot survive in this environment, and participating in this habit will spell death for your ministry. Some things are worth being falsely accused for. Innocent until proven guilty puts the burden of evidence on the accusers, which is honest. But guilty until proven innocent puts the burden of proof on the accused, a trap they may never escape.

- Control by controversy- Your church will not move forward in constant controversy. Those who stir up controversy will continue to do so unless they repent or move on. If a group does not like where the church is going, starting fires that the pastor must put out is a way to control the forward progress of the church. It is toxic to new people and will poison the efforts of those who are trying to revitalize the church.

- Control by manipulation- The parties that participate in this will manipulate people, conversations, and words to try to use them to leverage you. This person is extremely dangerous; they will try to get you to do things and say things that will be used as political leverage or to fuel accusations. They are the ones that attempt to turn the sheep against the shepherd. They must convince others that you are something you are not, so they can turn people against the person they painted you as and not the true you. This is the tactic the devil used on Eve in the garden of Eden, where he painted God as a liar, evil, and withholding something good from them.

- Control by finances- This is a common one. Money is a tool and is used to coerce the pastor. It has been said, those who control the purse control the institution. In our church, we made our budget as flexible as possible to alleviate the use of this tool as much as possible.

- Control by association- They turn others against the leader and demonize not only the leader but those who will not disown him, pressuring people to disassociate with him. (Us or you)

You will notice a rift that has developed between the old culture and the new as the church starts to grow. In church revitalization, your aim is to bring the old culture into a culture that will grow and become healthy enough to shine a light to your community, but this is extremely difficult to achieve. If you see a rift forming in the church, the political machine has been started, and your time is running out. You should attempt to bridge this rift and encourage parties from both sides to reconcile to the other. I know I always looked for ways to bring the two rifts together in my situation. However, the old culture side will continue to shrink as the new culture grows if they will not cooperate. If things do not change, this old culture will eventually pit itself against the new culture, make a list of demands, and if those demands are not met, they will cause a split.

You will then see those who are either new to the church or original but part of the new culture put under a lot of stress and pressure. When the old culture rejects the new, the environment will become toxic, and families and people part of the new culture will recognize they are not wanted and will want to leave. When the old culture decides to turn against the new, they are fueling the political machine, and you need to be ready. Though you should never enter a church to start a war, one will be started with you in this environment. You must not fight this war and return assaults when they assault you. Stay above the war, and act on biblical principles. Do not return anger for anger but continue to do good in the face of evil committed against you.

> "The servant of the Lord must not quarrel, but must be gentle toward all people, able to teach, patient, in gentleness instructing those in opposition. Perhaps God will grant them repentance to know the truth, and they may escape from the snare of the devil, after being captured by him to do his will."[21]

At this point, many people will think you didn't communicate enough. You weren't patient enough. Many interpretations are given

---

[21] 2 Timothy 2:24-26 MEV

to these circumstances; let me go on the record and say this type of divisive behavior in the church is sinful. Pastors are not politicians who are to make everyone happy, and to portray that image is irresponsible and causes many pastors to leave the ministry thinking they failed when they did the right thing. This happens when someone tries to justify such sin in the church and blame the pastor. The deeds of the flesh listed in Galatians 5 mentioned earlier are the root cause of such behavior. A double standard is at work when we condemn the sin of morality and justify the sin of divisiveness, and we differentiate between the sins of the church. We shun the idolatry of liberal theology with its acceptance of sinful behavior while making the idolatry of contentious behavior comfortable, asking our pastors to yield to the horror of it. Here is the list again.

hatred, strife, jealousy, rage, selfishness, dissensions, heresies, envy,[22]

- Hatred: Strong Negative Reaction; a feeling toward someone considered an enemy, possibly indicating volatile hostility.[23]
  - o Not agreeing with someone may lead to rejection or even parting ways, but hatred is revealed in active hostility to bring the demise of their adversary, stain their reputation, or even character assassination.
- Strife: This means those who practice strife, quarrel, especially rivalry, contention, and wrangling.[24]
  - o This is the competing nature of the fleshly mind. It finds its source in the ego of someone who refuses to lose and is determined to win against opponents. It views others as contenders to be conquered, not congregants for cooperation.

---

[22] Galatians 5:20b-21a MEV

[23] McWilliams, Warren 2003. "Hate, Hatred." In The Holman Illustrated Bible Dictionary, 723. Nashville: Holman Bible Publishers.

[24] Vine, W. E. 1981. "Strife." In The Vine's Expository Dictionary of Old and New Testament Words. Volume 4, 82. Old Tappan: Fleming H. Revell.

- Jealousy: which means to be jealous and zeal.[25]
  - o This fuels hostility when someone feels that someone else has an advantage and vigorously attempts to remove it.
- Rage: Hot anger and passion[26]
  - o This one explains itself.
- Selfishness: This word denotes ambition, self-seeking, rivalry, self-will being the underlying idea in the word; hence it denotes party-making. It is derived from erithos, meaning they will seek and win followers and create factions and sects.[27]
  - o This word points to the motives of the rivalry, that being, as some translations translate it, selfish ambition. This is the case when someone is convinced they will have their way, forms parties or sects, and attempts to divide the group and bolster their cause against the group they disagree with. This can lead to my side vs. your side instead of our side being God's side.
- Dissensions: literally division or standing apart or putting asunder.[28]
  - o This is the mentality of "them or us," as described later in the book when the divisive individual has caused division. It is when a person is unwilling to embrace another group and divides themselves and others from them.
- Heresies: denotes a choosing, choice. Then, that which is chosen, and hence, an opinion, especially a self-willed

[25] Vine, W. E. 1981. "Jealous." In The Vine's Expository Dictionary of Old and New Testament Words. Volume 2, 273. Old Tappan: Fleming H. Revell.

[26] Vine, W. E. 1981. "Wrath." In The Vine's Expository Dictionary of Old and New Testament Words. Volume 4, 239. Old Tappan: Fleming H. Revell.

[27] Vine, W. E. 1981. "Faction." In The Vine's Expository Dictionary of Old and New Testament Words. Volume 2, 68. Old Tappan: Fleming H. Revell.

[28] Vine, W. E. 1981. "Sedition." In The Vine's Expository Dictionary of Old and New Testament Words. Volume 3, 336. Old Tappan: Fleming H. Revell.

opinion, is substituted for submission to the power of truth and leads to division and the formations of sects. Such erroneous opinions are frequently the outcome of personal preference or the prospect of advantage. Which often leads to ruin.[29]

- o When we think of heresies, we think of people of opposing doctrine, but actual heresy comes from those who have refused to submit to the truth revealed in scripture, create a truth of their own liking, and causes a divide over the truth they have created that has very little to do with the truth found in scripture. These "heresies" are usually found in designing religion for personal preference over biblical truth, and yes, this can be found in the liberal and traditional camps.

- Envy: is the feeling of displeasure produced by witnessing or hearing of the advantage or prosperity of others; an evil sense is always attached to this word.[30]

- o This is the feeling that will cause good people to do bad things. When they feel someone has an advantage over them, they decide to bring the other person down instead of making themselves better.

The final symptom

One of the final symptoms of a revitalization rejection and tension rising is an odd interest in the church's status, such as the membership, financial and ministerial status, and the place of those who attend. They are measuring the political hill they will have to climb. This is why you do not take this on without changing

---

[29] Vine, W. E. 1981. "Heresy." In The Vine's Expository Dictionary of Old and New Testament Words. Volume 2, 217. Old Tappan: Fleming H. Revell.
[30] Vine, W. E. 1981. "Envy." In The Vine's Expository Dictionary of Old and New Testament Words. Volume 2, 37. Old Tappan: Fleming H. Revell.

the culture. You will not survive by yourself in congregational churches, only the congregation can shut this down, and if you do not have them behind you, you might as well start looking elsewhere.

CHAPTER TEN

A House Divided-When the Culture Turns Toxic to Growth

_____

As the tensions rise in the church from the rejection of the new culture by the old, you as the pastor will have a decision to make. As much as you love this church and know they are great Christian people, you will need to weigh the consequences of this situation on you, your wife, your family, and your ministry. Better to lose a church than to lose your ministry. Better to lose a church than your family. Better to lose a church than your peace of mind.

At this time, a lot was going on in my own heart. I made a decision that I thought I would never make. I stopped trying to grow my church. We no longer invited others to our church. I felt awful for the people dealing with the brunt of the pressure and problems, especially the people I brought in. We were so torn apart by a war that had nothing to do with Jesus; it had everything to do with the control of an institution. This was not a war I wanted to be in, and I realized this was the war that had been going on in the church for years. I would have removed my children, but the teachers and most in the church were still outstanding.

The culture will start to become poisoned by this sect. Please note that most in the church are casualties, not instigators of problems. Only a few will create toxicity in the church. You will work hard to understand this sect and try to love them into cooperation patiently, but if they are not receptive, then these efforts will be limited if not in vain. Nonetheless, the new culture will be tested as old political practices are being exercised to pollute the new culture. Problems will change dynamics as they move from minor, petty common occurrences to more significant, more intense issues. They are turning up the heat, this is not their first rodeo, and the political machine is accelerating

At this point, you need to decide if it is worth the war. Personally speaking, my wife had an emotional breakdown and wanted to resign as pastor's wife. We placed a date on the calendar that we would leave if things didn't change. It was six months. I was no longer interested in saving this institution but the church within it. We debated several options and even thought about looking for another ministry to serve, though I was ready to leave the ministry for a few years.

Your decision needs to be made with a lot of prayer. These wars taint the reputation of Christ, and many pastors have understandably left at this point to avoid the war. These wars will have a lot of casualties, but they shouldn't be because of you; keep your integrity. We each will answer to Jesus, you for you, they for themselves. You do what is right regardless of their choice of actions or words. Here are some elements of assessment as you pray over your possible departure.

Assess God's will for your church

There comes a time in the lifecycle of the church that you need to ask God if you are keeping something alive that He is removing the candlestick of. By the way, the candlestick refers to Christ speaking to the church at Ephesus when they abandoned the love and works they had at first, and Christ was on the verge of eliminating their place as a church. Here is the verse:

Remember therefore from where you have fallen. Repent, and do the works you did at first, or else I will come to you quickly and remove your candlestick from its place, unless you repent.[31]

When this happens, you need to ask the honest question: Is God removing their candlestick? If God is choosing to remove their candlestick, don't blame yourself. It wasn't the prophet's fault that Israel turned from God. They were faithful, you remain faithful. In your prayers, examine yourself with the accountability of godly men. You are human, and accountability to men who love Jesus will prove beneficial to you and your church.

Assess yourself and your family

Do you have enough left in you to take this on? Yes, you can do all things through Christ who strengthens you, but certain wars are not worth fighting. Assess your call. Is God asking you to bear through this, or is He permitting you to leave? You need to stay in tune with the Holy Spirit, not only to know when it is time to call it quits but to bear the spiritual load that will be placed on you. Burnout has many side effects, and people lose their ministries not only because of burnout but the effects of burnout in their lives. Be watchful and know that Satan will look for ways to take you out at these times of tremendous pressure. Better to lose the battle and win the war. Also, note that your family feels these pressures. My kids are still young, and only one will probably remember when daddy had drama at the church. I know good men who loved Jesus get chewed up, spit out, and never tasted meaningful ministry again. Also, assess your motives and choose not to enter the battle but to stand on biblical principles and not move. Do not allow the tools that controlled the previous pastors to be used on you. If you have the spiritual stamina for this, then move on to the following assessment.

---

[31] Revelation 2:5 MEV

Assess your leadership

In facing these rising tensions, you need to know that you would never target someone for their ill if your intentions are pure. You will continue to pray for reconciliation and cooperation. However, you will be the target when the next phase kicks in. Do strong leaders surround you that you know you can trust to stick with you through this dilemma? These situations cause good people to flee, and drama kills churches and is killing the one you are pastoring. Solid and honest leaders give confidence to their people, and you and they must love their church enough to stay and work through the coming storm.

I know for me, God had brought leaders into the church that faced this with me head-on and bore the load that came from the controversy. Many believe that the task of revitalization is too much for one man and only should be handled by teams that go in so as not to overburden one man and his family. This is wise, but that is why you do not "confront" the wrong at the beginning of this process but build a healthy culture with healthy leaders so when the controversy does break out, your healthy leadership will bear the load with you.

Assess your people

You need to do what is best for your people. Your goal is to see them living and serving in a Christ-centered community of believers built on the bible and the love of God. When this was rising in my church, I thought of all the wonderful people who were or were going to be caught in the middle of this war waged against me and the new culture. I thought of those who may never speak to me again because of the onslaught of accusations and condemnations on my reputation. I thought of the spiritual damage that would be done by another war waged in this church. I would not want to be the one standing before Jesus answering for this war. On the other hand, if these wonderful people leave this church and find healthy churches to be in, then I still did my job.

If you choose to leave...

If you choose to leave, I get it. These situations are stressful and can wreak havoc on the life of you and your family. I hope that you bathed it in prayer and know for sure that God led you away. But like Esther, perhaps you are there for such a time as this.

Another option: attempt to diffuse the situation and offer another chance to move forward

After having tried to work through the difficulties, you can try to move forward with the healthy culture and give them a chance to taste what a healthy culture is like. My wife and I had the incredible privilege to be part of healthy church cultures before and while at bible college. We thought if we could give them a chance to experience a healthy culture, they would see that church doesn't have to be wars but righteousness and peace and joy in the Holy Spirit. So, you can attempt to change the vocabulary and leadership dynamics of the church. In churches where administrative bodies are turned into authoritarian bodies that no longer follow the intent, definitions, or outlines in the constitution; many times the language used in those church governments, where the definitions have taken on a new meaning over the years, is so entrenched in tradition that it is hard to use those terms with proper definitions either by the bible, a dictionary or Robert's Rules of Order.

We took a small sabbatical that summer determined to decide to stay or leave and visited our former church. I came back with a plan that I felt God gave me. I was going to bring the congregation together under healthy practices and a renewed vision for the church. I would move forward under biblical principles and invest in the church's healthy culture instead of catering to the unhealthy. I would focus on the healthy, if not for anything else, my own sanity. I chose to stop showing up to the court hearings of the old culture, and I was no longer going to subject myself or the new culture to the old. So, I presented my leadership summit and called all the leaders to embrace where we were going, which went great. The congregation was on board, and now to see if these individuals would accept the new culture.

I was doing my best to operate under the constitution. Like I said before, these constitutions can become lengthy, complicated, contradicting, and subject to constitutional priests. So, I took a risk and communicated to the church that I would use a new vocabulary that emphasized the kind of administration granted by the constitution. So, though we would be using different terms, I was working by constitutional definitions instead of working with constitutional terms with definitions defined by the previous culture. Therefore, everything was going to be operated as usual, but we were going to adopt a new vocabulary that reinforced a team and family atmosphere and hopefully move the church from an "I say, you do" mentality to a "let's do this together" mentality.

Then I prayed and prayed and prayed that the old church culture would see that they were welcome to join the culture that the church was going to have. I interceded for the church that God would grant mercy and save the life of this church. I begged God to leave the candlestick in place and reignite a fire on its top. I pleaded with God to soften the hearts of the objectors and place in them a love for God, His church, and His mission. We saw a new excitement in the church, and I thought we had successfully brought the old culture into the new and avoided a potential disaster. If you choose to do this, you need to realize the risk you are taking because you are no longer allowing the old culture to define the parameters of the church. You will have done a ton of research and exegeted the scriptures and constitution if you are like me.

What should you include in this effort? I will tell you what mine had, but the whole meeting was to institute healthy ministerial practices in the church.

- An apology for not communicating enough and not being clear enough about the vision.
- Define what kind of cultures hurt churches
- Define what kind of cultures lead churches to victory and define what winning looks like for our church
- Revamped the church's vision and made it more ministry practical.
- We simplified the administration:
  - To be more reflective of the constitution (by the new vocabulary).
  - We removed extra control constructs that had been culturally put in place to allow leaders the freedom they needed to exercise their ministries and not to have to "get permission" to fulfill their ministries
  - To distribute authority back to its rightful place, namely the directors (team leaders) and the congregation, with a healthy view of pastoral leadership.
  - A re-emphasis on team leadership instead of an authority board.
- A Liberating service experience where I outlined the parameters of ministry, namely that ministries:
  - Functioned as a ministry and with the church
  - Stayed within budget
  - Stayed within biblical, legal, and ethical boundaries
  - Was in line with the vision of the church.
- Then I stated that my goals were S.I.M.P.L.E. for the leaders:
  - S- Satisfying: We want your service to be fulfilling both to your call and you.

- o I- Important: Every position and everything you do is important and matters to the Kingdom of God and the mission of this church.
- o M- Mine: We understand that this is your service to God, and we want you to have ownership over your ministry without being dictated.
- o P- Praiseworthy: Your ministry serves as an avenue to praise and worship Jesus
- o L- Linked in: Your ministry is linked together with the rest of the church to accomplish the larger purpose of God for the church
- o E- Enjoyable: We want serving God to be something you enjoy and do so joyfully for Jesus.
- Then I challenged everyone to be "ALL IN," and we did a leadership huddle and shouted our vision statement.

What can you expect? Well, those leaders and church members that are trying to move forward with you will be ecstatic. This will go over very well in most healthy churches, and this worked well for us. Perhaps this will aid in bringing the church forward and moving into a healthier culture. On the other hand, if the old culture refuses to move forward, this will broaden the gulf between the new and old cultures. I wasn't ready to give up on this church and wanted to give it my best shot to move forward before we decided to depart.

After working with this culture for some time, you have made every attempt to bring the church into a healthy culture; sometimes, those who refuse to move from the unhealthy culture will be preparing for their last attempt to bring the church back. Like I said in the previous section, if they have not come aboard, they are fueling the political machine that brought previous pastors down or at least subjugated them. The avenues of control in chapter nine will now be used with more intensity to either subjugate the pastor or destroy his ministry. That is the topic of the next chapter.

CHAPTER ELEVEN

Playing with Matches- The Point of Decision for the Old Culture

---

I n this process, accusations can be extreme and tiresome, but there comes the point if the old culture refuses to join the new, they will make their final move. This move is calculated, and they are prepared to see it through to the end. The old culture, now secluding themselves off of the church's main body, decides to take one last shot at bringing the church back into their possession, and usually, they are successful. They reject the new culture; they reject the new people; the church no longer feeds the unhealthy practices; it is time for their Hail Mary pass.

A coup is formed against the pastor (I am using political language because these are political maneuvers.) The problem with politics in the church is they are often corrupt both on the side of the contentious and the pastor who reacts poorly to poor politics. I cannot stress enough that you are not doing your church any favors by playing the games of politicians in the body of Christ. This coup will attempt to show itself larger and more intimidating than it really is. They will exaggerate problems and try to show their movement is large enough that the pastor must heed their demands.

Up to this point, many things have been used as potential leverage against the pastor, but now the full-blown ultimatum comes. These ultimatums can consist of accusations spanning everything from finances, church government, morality, legal grounds, etc. really anything they feel is extreme enough to bring the pastor down. At this time, you will be thankful for the boundaries you kept while at the church when approached to convince you to take risks with money, leaders, people, etc. You'll be thankful for the transparency you established in the leadership, and you'll be grateful for those with whom you have surrounded yourself. When the ultimatum comes, first, take a deep breath. You are going to need it.

Before I deal with this topic specifically, a couple of questions need to be answered. Is this biblical?... No. Is this honest?... No. Is this healthy?... No. Is this noble?... No. This is corrupt politics where coercion is the goal, not cooperation. Here are the avenues used to control the pastor again. For further description, please see chapter 9.

- Control by Intimidation
- Control by accusation
- Control by controversy
- Control by manipulation
- Control by finances
- Control by association

Hopefully, you have been building relationships with your people and should understand where the people are at. Like listed before regarding how to handle criticism, follow the same practice. This very well could be the warning shot to the pastor that he surrenders or pay the price. Here is the outline again:

- Is the criticism true or factual, or is it just emotion?
  o If true, how can you correct it?

- o How can you keep from making the same mistake again?
  - o If emotion, please to the next step.
- What is the motive of the criticizer?
  - o Is the criticizer open to being corrected?
  - o Are there demands behind the criticism that are unreasonable?
  - o Does a threat accompany the criticism?
  - o Is there an agenda that they want to achieve?
- Is the criticism in line with the scriptures?
  - o What is the verse?
  - o How can we be more biblical?

If it is true, then you need to repent and apologize. But you need to correct this unhealthy approach to solving this dilemma. It is incredibly harmful to think one person or a small group can destroy your ministry if they get angry. Tell them that others will be involved in the situation for accountability. You should never feel like your job is on the line all the time.

You need to follow the process if it is false or grossly exaggerated, especially combined with an ultimatum, which will reveal the individual's motives.

- Is the criticizer willing to be corrected with facts or explanations where they may have misunderstood something? If not, then you need to find out their true motive.
- If the accusations can only be corrected by giving into a list of demands that violate the Bible, the constitution, or your integrity, then the motive is now ulterior, and such demands are unreasonable.
- If the accusations are accompanied by a threat, an ultimatum that coerces you into surrender, then you acknowledge the possibility of sin and move from this step to the next, which moves into the biblical process of reconciliation.

- Is their accusation biblical? If the answer is no, then begin the process of Matthew 18, which starts with a private conversation between the two of you after a time where you searched your heart about wanting to see restoration and peace.

If this conversation does not reconcile the differences and the individual refuses rational reconciliation with facts and reality, then move on to the next step. This takes your relationship from private to public. It has a way of turning on a light in a dark situation and exposing sin in possibly both parties.

After the initial conversation with the individual, seek 1 or 2 witnesses that are mature and will be objective between you and the other party.

- Be prepared to emphasize your goal at reconciliation both with them and those they claim to represent (ask for names that you may reconcile with the group), your readiness to hear the explanations of the ultimatum, your love for the individual and the church, to answer accusations, apologize where you went wrong and to clarify the reality of the situation so that reconciliation has the best chance at happening.
- I had notes, so I knew what I wanted to say outside of the possible emotions that could occur. Since the accusations referenced a particular document, I researched the document and shared my findings.
- These witnesses could save your ministry if the accusations are false and the individual has ulterior motives. Some view this as extreme, but I believe Jesus knew that it would be these witnesses that could save the ministry and reputation of the innocent party.

If the person is sincere about their accusations and perceptions and is eager to reconcile, this should end the process. If the person has motives outside of reconciliation that are not met by reconciliation efforts on your part, then this will cause them to go the rest of the way and expose what their real agenda is.

This process is not standard in churches today because of our American values over biblical values. We have built tribes that see Matthew 18:15-20 as more offensive than just embracing the poor behavior and sometimes abuse. But, these situations and sinful habits continue (and become deeply rooted) because pastors refuse to follow the biblical outline of discipline. Unfortunately, some choose the path of least political resistance and are disobedient to our role as pastors in the scriptures. This process is suitable for dealing with unhealthy practices and ending ultimatums with poor motives. Unfortunately, some in the church will value emotion over facts, perception over reality, and peace at all costs. But it is the absence of the biblical process of reconciliation which allows these unhealthy cultures and practices a breeding ground both in the church and the lives of those who entertain them. Then we wonder why these in the church are the way they are.

Unfortunately, often the accuser will react poorly to the reconciliation effort and lead to Nero's fire. Under the emperorship of Nero, a large fire was started, and then blame was placed on the Christians. This led to widespread persecution of believers. This party may, in like manner, start a fire that will be pinned on the pastor. A fire is a controversy so considerable that it can destroy the pastor's ministry and possibly the church's. This is called character assassination. The attempt will be made to spread further slander to taint the leader's reputation, bolster their support, and convince others of their stance. If the motive was to coerce the pastor and regain possession of the church, then any resolution outside of that end will result in an unrestrained political onslaught.

You will be brought before the court of public opinion, as one accusation is hurled after another- painting you as anything they feel is strong enough to remove you. This resembles the Pharisees in their treatment of Jesus. It didn't matter if what they said was true; all that mattered was they wanted Jesus out of the picture. What fuels this? Probably many things, but particularly the sins mentioned at the book's beginning. This is disgusting but is often the occurrence of contentious churches. This is not a misunderstanding; this is sin. You do not have to worry about answering accusations that aren't true.

This will lead to a lot of repercussions and your choice of action I want to touch on. As for you, do not fight this war. You cannot win against someone willing to falsely accuse you, lie or pervert reality to garner support. By entering further political battles, you are only giving them further ammunition. A servant of the Lord must not quarrel but be gentle. Do not return insult for insult. Be kind, be gentle and let your character disprove their words. All who live godly will suffer persecution.

Here are some perspectives

- The rebellion and political machine will be full throttle to campaign to remove you as a pastor, make you so miserable that you will leave, or cause the church to fail. All stops have now been pulled because the attempt to usurp the congregation and coerce the pastor to pull the church back into their possession has failed.

- Church members and community members will be called and met privately to convince them of the accuser's position and infiltrate other relationships in the church. Your relationships with your people are vital. This is because the accuser is trying to show that more people were against the pastor than just their small group. Again, some of these people will leave because of pressure from the accusing parties, believing their accusations or avoiding drama.

Most people do not leave because of direct opposition to a pastor but more indirect opposition through the accusing party.

- You see this behavior reflected in the trials and execution of Jesus. The Pharisees worked up the crowds to bolster support; they falsely accused, twisted Jesus' words, and lied to remove Him.

- The levels of transparency you created earlier in your ministry will prove crucial as leaders and volunteers will scour the emails to see if what was said was true. Without these efforts to create transparency on your part, they would have no reason to question the accusations of your attackers. I printed them out, prepared to read them in front of the congregation. Your accuser will most likely not show up to a public forum where information is readily available.

- You will see the absence of church members who bought into the false accusations or were part of the old culture. Always be willing to talk to people, but this is often of no avail. Also, offer the witnesses to those willing to hear.

- Be prepared for the social media backlash of people who were told false accusations. Again, correct the charge, offer to speak privately, offer the witnesses, and kindly inform them that such social media attacks on your accounts will be deleted in the future.

- Collateral damage- the group that opposes you will most likely be small, but the collateral damage will be significant because people hate drama and hate being put in the middle. Drop the rope of tension on your end and just appreciate that they are still part of your life and the church.

- Don't participate in the war and refuse to participate in the same sin that is being waged against you. Even if you lose the church, your sleep will be sweet. Remember what Paul said,

> *"17 Repay no one evil for evil. Commend what is honest in the sight of all men. 18 If it is possible, as much as it depends on you, live peaceably with all men. 19 Beloved, do not avenge yourselves, but rather give place to God's wrath, for it is written: "Vengeance is Mine. I will repay," says the Lord. 20 Therefore "If your enemy is hungry, feed him; if he is thirsty, give him a drink; for in doing so, you will heap coals of fire on his head."*
>
> *21 Do not be overcome by evil, but overcome evil with good.*[32]

- As a church, reach out to the accuser and be friendly, but your time needs to be spent loving your flock that stayed. Don't let the issues of those who left keep you from loving your flock that stayed. They are hurting, and though they may not have seen the ugliest parts, they feel the repercussions. Take care of their wounds and allow God to heal yours.

- How you react will be vital. Do not react; just act with which you already know. Do what is right and in line with God's Word. Allow God to take care of the consequences.

- In the end, my relationships with my people and pastors around the community led to my staying and healing and were instrumental in the church's survival. Having these connections also informed me of what the accusations were against me and the actions of the accusers. Other pastors were even willing to come to my church and testify of those actions to save our ministry. I am a blessed man. God was already preparing for this before I was.

---

[32] Romans 12:17-21 MEV

Prepare to take some time to heal with your church. There will be those who will struggle and be confused by the actions of this sect; your continued presence and patience will help them heal. Some will be like a healing balm for you too. Your church will never be the same, which is not necessarily a bad thing.

Cease from anger, and forsake wrath; do not fret- it only causes harm.[33]

---

[33] Psalm 37:8 NKJV

CHAPTER TWELVE

Observations of How This Happens in our Churches

B efore I go on to the next chapter, I want to answer the question... why? What brings churches to this point? How do churches get to the point where they are more known for their contention than the light they shine? I cannot say that I know everything there is to know. Still, I can give you some of my observations with my interpretations, that paired with other men who have experienced similar things, will paint a more precise and clearer picture of how these churches were cursed with contention.

My first observation is that the contentious are usually good people. Someone recently asked me if I was as angry at the controversial people as they were with me. My answer is no; I am not angry. I am not angry because I can understand the difficulty and contention they felt within their own heart about losing control of an institution they loved. This institution was becoming something they didn't want it to become. This institution, their position, and other traditions had become so intertwined with their identity that when I (or any other pastor) attempted to move the church in any direction, I was challenging their identity.

The problem was they didn't have a healthy faculty of realizing this dilemma in their own heart and coping with the reality of their mindset. So, the bad man was the one that made them feel this way, not that they had an unhealthy attachment to tradition, position, authority, or a building. Not only that, but when working with the members that proved to be contentious, the contention usually spawned from a level of immaturity which led to an unhealthy resolution process in their own hearts. I don't mean that as a put-down. Still, when church officers cannot even tell you where to find the qualifications and descriptions of their office in the bible when they try to define church structure by tradition or resort to unbiblical politics, we must ask why the bible is so foreign to these offices and those who fill them? My answer: because they were novices and fell into the category Paul warned about in 1 Timothy 3:6.

I have four kids, and I work with my kids on developing healthy thought processes, communication, and resolution practices that help them grapple with their emotions and thoughts and experiences so they can make sense and use these faculties and grow in them. That is why communication is vital to the parent-child relationship because you are helping them formulate the mindset they will have for the rest of their lives. The people who cause these types of problems are born into the church where tradition has defined Christianity for them; they have never been discipled nor taught to read their bible regularly, which leaves them with minimal resources to draw from in answering the questions of faith, its church, its leaders and its purpose. Like a child still learning why lying is so bad and hurts people, so are those young in the faith and still do not understand the damage caused by dissension and sins of like manner.

I can say this because I grew up in this setting. I was in church almost all my life, and I had very little to no experience with my bible; how I defined my faith was things I had heard from the pulpit or people I respected or things I experienced at "my" church. My faith was tied up in my church, and it wasn't until I lost my church that I realized that I wasn't as founded on Jesus as I thought. I hated losing my church when it split (I was 18), but it led me to take responsibility for my growth and surround myself with those like-minded that I cleared up the why, the who, the how, the what of my faith and ministry. In my years, I have seen some that were still very much spiritual children, and they acted like children with temper tantrums and all, not realizing the devastating effects it had on those around them. This is the fruit of making converts without making disciples and building tribes instead of churches. The previous generation emphasized the "say the prayer, sit down and tithe" mentality. Even today, we see the emphasis of ministry as filling a box with faces instead of a community of growing disciples. You will always have people young in the faith at your church; just don't put them into leadership.

So, why are people in the church still spiritual infants? Many reasons, one being pastors do not always preach the whole counsel of God, many times resorting to sermons that make people happy, not holy. The second is the value system of the church. People do not value spiritual growth; they value church attendance and other cultural expectations. We spend more time emphasizing that people should attend and not enough time thinking of the substance they will receive if they do attend. Christianity is not organically an institutional religion; it is a lifestyle religion that results in community. Each person has chosen to follow Jesus, and this new relationship leads them to grow personally and brings them into a community of other like-minded committed disciples. In our era, we deal with the fruits of a time when people were won to church but not to Jesus.

Another observation is we allow our ego to lead us to take possession of the church where we will not hand over "our" church to someone else, even the next generation. We would rather see it die than lose control of "our" church. This same ego also keeps us from searching the scriptures to define our faith, and we pull ourselves out of the submission to the scriptures to bow to the opinions and preferences of our minds and traditions. The next thing we know, we have churches saying all the right words with little fruit because the fruit comes from meaning, not just words. You can say all the right words in the correct order. Still, as long as you define them by something other than the bible, rather by tradition or contemporary culture, both are idols, and we are guilty of committing idolatry.

The bible becomes something we carry but do not read, something we honor but do not use. We redefine offices in the church by cultural values; we will appoint someone who may not be biblically qualified, but they are there three times a week, shovel the walks in the winter, mow the grass in the summer and thus are put into position. Then when some pastor comes along and believes the bible is welcome there, they will not receive it; they have possibly been Christians longer than he has been alive; what does he know? This leads me to the following reason this circumstance comes up. The Word of God has lost its centrality and authority in the church.

When facing all the opposition, not one time was a bible pulled out by the old culture. Bibles are often shut right in front of pastors; I know it has happened to me. Now, I don't mean to paint these individuals as awful because the Word of God is confronting at times. However, if a church is not comfortable reading, searching, and heeding the scriptures, it points to a deeper problem. The scriptures are the revelation of the centerpiece of our faith: Jesus, yet they become the ornament of our faith. They are meant to be the core of our faith and yet become peripheral. The bible is the toolbox to ministry, and yet we treat it as figuring, something nice to claim but not to heed. If our faith was a vine, the trunk of that vine is Jesus and His Word with us as branches where we produce fruit by Jesus. Yet we make the Word a branch of the trunk of our Christianity made up often of tradition, rituals, and memorials and wonder why we have no fruit.

The gospel becomes a tool to grow our church instead of to change the lives of those who come. The faith becomes self-focused and self-serving as we design our church. Slowly but surely, if we do not keep returning to the book, we will replace it with what we like. We hammer sins that we find disgusting yet overlook those that often plague our churches. We slowly redefine our church according to our culture's priorities and values, and when the culture outside changes, we still want to emphasize those values. The problem is, these values are not eternal and often have little to no scriptural support. So when I am older, if I am not careful, I will try and push the values of my culture that I have allowed to define my Christianity onto the next generation. They will read the bible and recreate the situation we have today. I will do things that fly in the face of scripture in the name of my values and traditions. Pair that with an ego that can't lose, and you have the potential for another disaster.

The truth is, I believe contentious churches have lovely people, with some of those people as those who have lost the centrality of the scriptures, have defined their identity by tradition, and have not heard, read, or heeded the whole counsel of God. They have not received the faith but taken ownership of it and allowed themselves to create an idol in their image according to their likeness. In this scenario, they are guilty of doing essentially the same thing as the liberals. They have dismissed scriptural teaching for that which is more palatable to them. Legalism and liberalism are two sides of the same coin. Both remove themselves from under the authority of the scriptures. Both create an idol that fits their values more so than the God of the bible. Both dictate what is true by their opinions and preference (see heresy in chapter two.) And both are equally as rebellious to the God they will meet. Again, we have been building tribes in many ways, not churches (see chapter two.)

When we die and meet God, we will not meet the God of your imagination. We will meet the God of the bible. As Christians, we need to stop being so confident that God is who I say He is but read again and again and again the revelation of God found in His scriptures. Asking for God to reveal more and more of Himself to us and that we would be humble enough to receive Him as who He is, not who we think He should be, or we may be just as guilty as the Pharisees worshiping a God they didn't recognize when He stood right in front of their faces.

Chapter Thirteen

Turn the Page and Start a New Chapter for Your Church

———

Turn the page and start a new chapter. There is a process that must take place to survive the storm. This is crucial to your survival as a minister and as a church. You and your church have just watched the plague that infects many of our churches do its damage at this point in your ministry.

The three D's to overcome

Damage-

One of the most challenging things I have seen for churches that go through this is watching a group of people attempt to usurp their own church for the sake of keeping it from moving forward. They would rather starve the church financially, continue to taint its reputation, and practically demolish its ministries than let go of their control. In my time at the church, I was adamant about respecting the church's heritage and never removed a ministry, never halted a tradition. Titus 2 teaches a multigenerational church. I encouraged the younger families to embrace the older and serve them because I didn't want a young church, primarily because the bible doesn't make room for it. But if the old culture will not embrace the new unless they can control the church, this will lead to damage. You will see the ministries of the former culture crumbled under the weight of the old-culture leaders, their hostile reactions and political maneuvers, or the people left discouraged from them. We want to revitalize these churches, but a new church is often built where the old church destroyed itself.

Like a torrential storm to a building built on sand, so catastrophe to a church built on tradition. Like an earthquake to an unstable structure, so a catastrophe to a church with unstable leaders. Like a city bombed by its former occupants, so disaster to a church which had become an empire of man. These events are followed by fallout when catastrophes rather in nature, politics, or the religious world. Trimmers follow earthquakes, floods follow Storms, wars are followed by famine, fires are followed by destruction, and so the wrath of some are followed by fallout.

The following year or so, while the smoke clears, will show what is left standing and what was demolished. During this whole process, you were challenging (many times without knowing) a dying empire. The dying empire will demolish itself before it surrenders. A church is not supposed to be the empire of those who lead it but the kingdom of Christ. And if Christ and His Word are not welcome there, you know it needs to repent.

During this time, you will continue to see the fallout. People will continue to leave either by pressure from those who left, the stress of rebuilding the ministry, or the biggest: discouragement and shock due to the destruction. People cannot wrap their minds around why people would do this; they will only have a part of the information and false information while trying to make sense of what just happened. Typical reactions include looking for someone to blame, running from the situation, and losing hope. They will not understand how people intentionally tried to destroy a church. But when a group of people demand that the church bow to them, they have put themselves as God, and not even the Lord of the church can correct them; they have an institution of man, not Christ. Call it what you will, but it's not Jesus's.

Ministries of the former church will most likely crumble because of the fallout and the discouragement of watching their church destroy itself. The people who choose to cause this much damage do not understand the damage they do to not only the pastor they don't like but the people they supposedly love. Jesus in John 10 says the hirelings flee when the wolf comes because they do not care about the sheep and the sheep are scattered. But the Good Shepherd stays and protects the sheep. If God has called you to shepherd that flock under Him, do not leave after an event where you did your job.

Be patient and understanding with the people you still have. You are still their pastor. Overlook their harsh comments and ridicules and sometimes interrogations as they mull over the reality of what just took place in their hearts. People will react poorly, overlook it. People will fall apart, be there willing to pick up the pieces with them. If your church is like mine, this is not the first time they have had to do this. Pray with them and for them while loving them. You are not their pastor only in the good times but also in the hard times. If you want them to stick with you, you must stick with them.

Disappointment-

The truth is we have expectations of others, and in situations that are as ugly as a contentious church can be, you will be very disappointed. There is something genuinely disappointing when individuals in our churches act more like those who killed Jesus than those who followed Him. In these situations, you will experience many disappointing characteristics, including but not limited to: false accusation, scheming, lying, politics, threats, ultimatums, extortion, sedition, character assassination, destruction of your ministry, reputation, and more. They may not murder you, but they will murder everything about you. That is one reason why Jesus equated hatred with murder.

What makes these situations even worse is who chooses to participate in the behavior. Many who decide to make a pastor their enemy are not those outside the church but inside. That is why we cannot ignore the other deeds of the flesh found in Galatians 5. The fact that these sins are practiced in a contentious church clearly shows rebellion. God has a very small place in many of their hearts, where power is the goal and politics is the game.

Discouragement-

These situations have a way of not only taking the wind out of your sails but ripping your sails to shreds. Just the other day, I heard of another pastor's marriage falling apart, and it all began with the discouragement of watching a church run him out. You just watched as years of your ministry were demolished by uncontrolled people. Even after the damage is done, many ministers cannot mentally handle all the carnage left. This is enough to break ministers. The discouragement can be monstrous, not just as you think of the war that took place but the process by which it will take to rebuild the ministry.

Let me tell you; you are not alone. You were called there to see this process through. Do not look at those who wanted to destroy you but look at those the Lord has entrusted you with. There will be a lot of unanswered questions, and it would be so much easier to walk away. But now is the time for you to stand up and lead the church forward. I would suggest surrounding yourself with voices that speak truth into your ears and with those who have done this before you. Great leaders are not made in ease but in difficulty, not by the selfish ambition of power but by the humiliation of sacrifice for those entrusted to your care. We are not entitled to easy ministries; Jesus didn't have one, and neither has most following after who was faithful.

Taking time to grieve and start new

One of my mentors always encourages me to grieve losses. If you avoid grieving, then you can't move on. In bible times, they would grieve loudly, uncontrollably, for extended times and often in affliction. Today we try to get over grief quickly or avoid it. Understand you need to embrace the depths of healthy grief and mourn these catastrophes but also understand that dealing with that grief will be the place you will find joy. A rebuilt city is a joy to those who saw it destroyed; a rebuilt house is a joy to those who saw it burn. Healing first must come from grieving, not dismissing hurt. You will live with scars that you will have for the rest of your life but do not live with wounds you wouldn't take time to treat and are still not healed, festering and torturing you and those around you.

Catastrophe doesn't have to be the end. Many believe disaster ends ministry, but it only ends that chapter of ministry. Even good faithful pastors will see catastrophe or controversy. Good pastors that do their work according to the scriptures will face difficulty. Some pastors succeed politically but dismiss principle; others succeed principally and do not allow politics to control them. Yes, the damage can be significant, but the outcome can be more significant. I am convinced that God did His work.

Did God answer my prayer to save the candlestick of my church? Yes, but not with the answer I was hoping for. The church today is not the church I was hired into. About six months after the drama, I brought in a former pastor of our church that I had gotten close to. When he showed up, he told me, "this isn't the same church I pastored." I knew then my answer to my prayer. On a side note, I believe we now see the church in the health and vibrancy that it once had many years ago. So, in a way, it was revitalized to its former place.

Was I rejoicing? No. I grieved and mourned and wept. I loved these people; that's not the issue. I prayed and interceded for this church. I went out of my way to exhort, love, and cherish this church. I preached my heart out to get them to see their church from the eyes of her Creator and Redeemer. I worked diligently to fulfill my call from the Scriptures, and I believe I did. I indeed made mistakes along the way, but this church did not deserve this. The choice was not whether I wanted them or not; the choice was whether they wanted God and His Word. Remember this; it is better to be rebuilding the first floor on a rock-solid foundation than sitting on the 10th floor of a building built on sand. So, as Proverbs 24:16 MEV states:

> For a just man falls seven times and rises up again, but the wicked will fall into mischief.

It's time to get back up and start again. I took a year to work through the grieving process, and God put people in my life that aided my healing. Some healing came from community members who had seen this happen at our church several times before and apologized to me and provided me some comfort. You have decided not to fight the war; you have decided to take time to heal; it is now time to decide to go at it again. Wipe the dust from your feet; it is time to move on. No one will fulfill your call for you, so embrace your call over their condemnation.

Rebuild on the Rock

You now have the opportunity to rebuild this ministry. As time goes on, the people will heal and grow past this. One of my most cherished moments was when a lady told me that she had invited her new neighbor. She told me that she didn't feel comfortable inviting people for the last number of years and thanked me for a church healthy enough that she felt comfortable inviting others to. Thank Jesus for His work in His church. These are the moments when you know it was all worth it. You now have a church that, instead of saying, "this is my church that will run my way," is saying, "This is God's church, and we want it to run His way." You could say this church was redeemed.

> *Therefore, if any man is in Christ, he is a new creature. Old things have passed away. Look, all things have become new.*[34]

Would you be content with your circumstances if you could remove the drama of the last few years and the hardship you faced? Let me explain; if someone came to me and told me, "Jonathan, I am going to give you a large facility, people you already have a relationship with to start a church and the finances to get you moving." I would be ecstatic! You have to view your church as new so that you can move forward from its past. Start doing your first works again because now those works will be even more fruitful with the congregation fully on board. Hopefully, this situation has brought your people closer, and they have decided to stick with the church. Treat the church as a new church and instead of throttling up a political machine, throttle up the ministry machine and go!

Start asking the questions of what can our church be? What does God want for our church? Make it a habit to talk about where you are going as a church. I would encourage you to study the scriptures again with your church and define the church purely according to the scriptures. I once preached a sermon called "Building Plans for the Local Church." As time goes on and a church lives out its lifespan, I am a huge advocate that pastors regularly go back to the building plans with their church. This is to make sure the direction of the church is still in line with the founding principles (the bible) and not drifting either into liberalism or traditionalism. It reminds the pastor, deacons, other leaders, and the congregation of their role, responsibility, and qualifications. It keeps the church faithful

---

[34] 2 Corinthians 5:17 MEV

to the building plans that God has ordained for his church. Staying true to the principles of scripture is an intentional endeavor and not happenstance. If you talk to anyone who builds houses, they will tell you the importance of staying true to the building plans and referencing them often. It maintains the integrity of the structure, the safety of those inside, and the longevity of its lifespan. As the building plans to a house being built, so the bible to a church being built.

Encourage the change of thinking from what we have been through to where we are going now. Start preaching the vision again and reignite the fire in that body of believers for God and His purpose for your church. Start to initiate a new legacy, not of drama, controversy, and contention; but of the bible, sincere love, generosity, and changing lives. This church DOES have a future! Continue to believe and proclaim that your church's best days are still ahead. A lady who attended my church many years before I arrived rebuked me for its controversy, saying it was a good church. I told her I agreed, but the church she once knew was not the church I walked into, but now the church can return back to its roots and the health it once had many years ago.

Build a healthy leadership structure

Rebuild a healthy leadership and ministerial structure with dispersed authority to the leaders for their ministries. If the congregation has installed them into those ministries, give them the authority to do their job. Create transparency in the leadership so that there isn't a new sect starting to operate the church. Make sure that the new leaders are qualified and be clear about expectations. It is more work but try to come up with service descriptions that include their responsibility, the channels of problem-solving, and opportunities to develop.

When looking for leaders, find ones that will cooperate. It

becomes very frustrating when a leader doesn't collaborate with other leaders and doesn't respect the areas of different ministries. If someone can't be a team player, do not put them on the team. Talent never replaces cooperation. Many talented people out there have a tremendous number of gifts and could do great things, but if they cannot work with others, their talents will only be so effective. Better a person with less talent willing to cooperate and grow than a person with a lot of talent who refuses to collaborate and grow.

Find leaders that will be realistic about the church's health biblically, legally, and ministerially. It can become very burdensome to deal with leaders who do not understand risk management and are unwilling to apply the precautions laid out by the church to protect itself. The church is only as protected as its weakest leader. You will never eliminate all risk, but to have a leader not willing to take any precautions to protect themselves and the church is as much a liability as an asset.

We decided to have an annual installation service where the church's vision would be preached with a call to integrity for the leaders. At the end of this book, I have placed a leadership covenant I created for the occasion (see resource C). I made it so that each leader would have to sign the covenant to serve on the team in front of the congregation for accountability.

Give your church some depth

When in college, I would love to see the excitement of a new bible college student as the school was equipping them with the tools necessary to dig into the word of God. I know that my experience at bible college deepened my hunger for the Bible and gave me the required utensils to feed that hunger. We started courses that did that for our people, and I saw them fall in love with the reading and study of the scriptures. The Bible came to life as we studied the people, context, and content of the word of God. By doing this, you are setting the pace for your church to grow broad and deep. These studies (and ones like them) will ground people into the purpose of the church. The more the Bible is opened, discussed, and preached, the more influence it will have.

Unfortunately, churches with an unhealthy culture and ministry also have an unhealthy diet in theology. The sermons may be nice, but shallow or the teachings may be wrong altogether. I remember becoming physically sick over what a pastor said from the pulpit, mainly that Jesus never made anyone unhappy and always made people happy and gave them what they wanted. The "have it your way" Christianity is not a new concept and has entitled some to think it must be their way.

Be clear about where the church is headed, but channel your energy, people, and resources to a few ministries to be productive instead of many busy ministries. It is time to build on the rock, and though this doesn't guarantee that your church will not have to weather a few storms, you know you can be confident about the foundation by which it's built. Challenges still lie ahead, but as a body of believers, you can move forward in your purpose as a church.

Emphasize personal responsibility

In the modern church, we have "the great delegation," which is the idea that since we have specialized offices in the church both locally and internationally, that exempts us from personal responsibility to the church or our community, outside of our financial contribution. If your church will see any meaningful impact in its community, you need to convince your church to take responsibility for its ministries. So many churches are convinced that if they have the right guy in the pulpit, their church will grow. It is also true that many churches are convinced that since we pay a person to minister, our duty is fulfilled in them. The pastor is not a politician who needs your financial support and vote. He needs your hands and feet to share the love of Jesus.

Ephesians 4, 1 Corinthians 12, Romans 12, etc., make it abundantly clear that the body of believers ministers to itself and those outside with their gifts and abilities. A church that has overcome the issue of contention still has a lot of work to do. It will take every part doing its share to see the body grow into its head: Christ. Hostility can be very discouraging, but so can apathy. You need to be honest with your congregation about their need to join in the effort. Just like you needed them to overcome the contentions, you will need them to jump on board and help in moving forward. Like a large boat with many people on it, if one person is paddling, you will not go far, but if everyone works together, heading in a good direction, the possibilities are limitless.

> *Therefore, since we are encompassed with such a great cloud of witnesses, let us also lay aside every weight and the sin that so easily entangles us, and let us run with endurance the race that is set before us. 2 Let us look to Jesus, the author and finisher of our faith, who for the joy that was set before Him endured the cross, despising the shame, and is seated at the right hand of the throne of God. 3 For consider Him who endured such hostility from sinners against Himself, lest you become weary and your hearts give up.*[35]

---

[35] Hebrews 12:1-3 MEV

RESOURCES

15 Commitments of the Revitalizer

Commitment #1- I will live by the Ethics, Virtues, and Values of Jesus

The first commitment you have to make in any ministry, especially revitalization, is living the values of Jesus. I will sum these up for you, but this is by no means exhaustive.

1. Truth Telling- I will not lie but tell the truth and be as honest as I know how.
2. Transparency- I will live blamelessly and not have another agenda that I hide from others.
3. Non-vengeance- I will not retaliate nor repay anyone evil for evil but overcome evil with good.
4. I will refrain my tongue from evil and choose to continue to speak the truth.
5. I will not allow the slander of others to define me or keep me from moving forward.

Commitment #2 Embrace the Challenge of Ministry

Life is full of challenges regardless of the path you take. How you respond to challenges will determine if you are successful in your endeavors. If you start a business, you will have to work through the challenges of gaining customers, keeping customers, turning a profit, market your service, budgeting your finances, etc. Ministry is the same; all ministries have their challenges, and only embracing those challenges will result in succeeding. If you are a person who runs from challenges or avoids challenging situations, you will have to change your mentality. Challenges are not reasons to give up but reasons to find creative solutions to meet those challenges.

The perk for you is you not only are choosing to embrace these challenges, but God also calls you to embrace these challenges. In a world where you are given a box to function in, you need to think outside of that box to remedy your challenges. The last few years of ministry have presented many challenges that we had to work through. Refuse to allow the norm to limit your choices in solving the challenges before you. For example, many church plants and revitalization efforts fail with the ending of funding. I didn't require funding. To give me more flexibility with the demands of ministry while also providing for my family, I started a small business where I could control the time and mold it around my needs. It worked for Paul, and it worked for me.

I was told on several occasions why I would fail. Of course, there is the risk of failure. But you have already failed if you do not try. (you saw that coming, didn't you!) Throughout this whole journey, you will be reminded of the real possibility of failure. As one of my mentors put it to me when I found out that I was not going to receive funding and was wondering if it was worth moving forward, "did God call you to this community *if* you received funding?" The answer was no. Does the call of God change because of the challenge that lies ahead? No. Success is found in obedience, not results. Allow the bible to set the trajectory of your ministry and be the boundaries of the solutions for your challenges. Keep your heart and mind open to solutions God will provide as you face various challenges. Ask God regularly for wisdom, pour over the scriptures and act in faith.

Commitment #3 Grow Up by Taking Responsibility for Your Maturity and Development

No one is going to get you out of bed, get you ready and hand you a ministry. If God calls you to serve Him in a specific capacity, you will have to obey that call. No one is going to do this for you. Many people attempt to move forward on the coattails of initiators, but only those who are willing to keep putting one foot in front of the other will see it through to the end. Maturity is taking responsibility for your life and development. Maturity is applying what you already know and being eager to learn more. Maturity sees failure as an opportunity to grow. Maturity keeps its eye focused and does not allow itself to get distracted by unimportant matters. Take responsibility for your biblical knowledge, time, and ministry development. Make reading and studying the bible a standard practice of your life. Surround yourself with mature individuals that will regularly stretch you and mold you. Keep your eyes on the prize of the high calling of God in Christ Jesus.

Commitment #4 You Were Not Called to Maintain an Institution

If you were called to plant or revitalize a church, you are called to see that church fulfill what God created it for. You are called to declare the word of God to those people. You are called to love them and equip them for ministry work. Essentially, your ministry has a purpose for more than just existence. Existence should always be tied to purpose and not the mere existence of an institution. The burden is not on you to maintain an institution; the responsibility is on the institution to define itself by God's purpose. An institution that is nothing more than an institution is a club, not a church. Put reminders of the "why" you are there, so you do not lose focus, fall into a routine, or leave in the middle of your ministry work.

Commitment #5 Stay Focused- Don't Get Distracted by Other Matters

There will always be something demanding your attention, time, and energy in ministry. As a steward of your life, do not allow just anything to use your resources. Redeem the time by focusing your personal resources in the direction God wants you to go. Shun busyness and ask the questions that will lead your life to be productive as a husband, father, and minister. Don't spend your time running in circles or into meetings but evaluate your life and the outcome you believe God wants for your life and adjust accordingly. Time spent away in prayer, retreat, and reflections are rewarded by better use of your time and energy. Your life is not found in doing everything but doing the right things. You do the right things when you focus on being the right person before God and allowing Him to structure your life. You may feel you need to be busy, but we often spin our wheels in the mud of life.

Commitment #6 Preventing Burnout by Keeping Healthy Relationships

Surround yourself with healthy relationships. You only have so much relational energy; if you are an introvert like myself, those resources can be low at times. When you have relationships that suck that energy out of you, you will not have enough left for those who deserve that energy. Look for healthy relationships that can create relational energy and pour back into you as you pour into them. You will always have people who will burn out your energy. It's okay to be a little picky about who you invest your time into. You can be acquainted with everyone but pour into those relationships that keep you relationally healthy, and you keep them relationally healthy. It's okay to have boundaries with wonderful people but run you dry either by drama, criticism, double standards, or demands.

Commitment #7 Prevent Burnout by Keeping Realistic Expectations

The second part of preventing burnout is boundaries on ministry. There will always be more to do. People will have expectations of you that are unrealistic. They don't see the time you put in, the people you work with, and the effort you put forth. They only see a limited amount of your life, so their vantage point is also limited. For the sake of your family, your personal life, and your sanity, please put boundaries in place. If you were wondering, it is okay to have a life outside of ministry. Everyone in your church has a life outside of their jobs and church and assuming that your life should be consumed with church activities and needs is unreasonable and will burn you out. What are the priorities that God has given you through His word? God is the one who gave you the time you have, and if you can't fit it all in, then maybe God is not asking you to do everything you're doing.

Commitment #8 Prevent Failure by Keeping Moral Boundaries

Even good men can have affairs, be sucked into porn, and make substantial life mistakes when they allow themselves to burn out and let their guard down. They become more susceptible to attacks from the evil one when weak. Keeping healthy moral boundaries might sound ridiculous to those who don't believe in them, but they will save your ministry and marriage while other people are falling apart. I can't tell you how often I was ridiculed for not regularly hugging women, not being alone with women, or limiting relationships with women to business or with my wife present. I have also been surprised at how many marriages have fallen apart because a spouse gave into temptation they allowed in their lives by the lack of boundaries. Faithfulness is not found in strength while immersed in temptation but a humble acceptance and understanding of your weaknesses.

Commitment #9 Encourage Members to be Participants, Not Just Spectators

According to Ephesians 4, pastors play a specific role in the church, accompanied by the rest of the body edifying itself in truth and love. Unfortunately, today for many of our pastors, the burden of carrying the traditional pastor load is unbearable and falls out. Each member plays a part according to First Corinthians 12, but the current model in many of our churches does not resemble it. Encourage the body's participation to edify itself, and those will share the load in it. In the last few decades, we have seen congregants delegate the church's work to the "hired workers," aka pastors, evangelists, missionaries. We need to delegate some of it back to the church.

Commitment #10 Always Work Yourself Out of a Job

When the work, effort, sacrifice all falls on one man, the failure of that man to bear that load will also lead to the failure of the ministry. A couple of years ago, I was challenged to "do more" because I was the pastor… I am only one man; I am the under-shepherd. Never allow yourself to be the irreplaceable piece. It's Christ's church; I am just a member fulfilling my role. You need to look for ways you are not required because you have maturing men and women underneath you. You want your church to be so spiritually mature that they are entirely competent to fill your shoes. You take care of God's church and let God take care of you through His church.

Commitment #11 Don't Define Yourself by the Pressure to Perform

Living up to everyone's "expectations" becomes the pastor's priority, knowing that he could lose them or the church if he doesn't. Regrettably, this creates an unhealthy relationship of politics that keeps the pastor from being the pastor in many ways. It also pressures the pastor to have values that "perform" rather than values that "honor."

The good news is that it doesn't have to be that way. I have chosen not to "work the system" and accept the traditional model, and I have taken some heat for it. But, on the flip side, our church emphasizes the scriptures on the role of the pastor and how he fits into the rest of the serving body. Over the last few years, I have heard, "we want a biblical church" being echoed back to me. So, the following few keys are ways that I have found efficacious in shifting the church back into the biblical direction.

Commitment #12 Look for Ways to Give Away Ministry

Straight up, I loved sharing my pulpit with the gifted teachers of my church. Realize that it is God's church, not your church. That means you will answer to God for your service and that you are not responsible for "all" the ministry in the church. Pray that God will give you the insight to give away ministry to the gifted people in your congregation. Also, challenge your members to "own" their ministry before God. Keep your hands off unless they cross biblical lines and watch them flourish.

Commitment #13 Take the Time to
Identify Gifts and Employ Them

Encourage people to jump in. Each has been given at least one gift to serve the church. *As everyone has received a gift, even so, serve one another with it as good stewards of the manifold grace of God.*[36] Make a spiritual gift survey part of your membership class, and don't be afraid to invite people to participate in different ministries in the church. The great men and women of God for tomorrow often start today with an opportunity to serve in ways they may find a bit intimidating.

Commitment #14 Don't Be Afraid to Let Ministries Fail

Here is a big one. Your church was not meant to handle all the ministries of larger churches. Usually, a church can only handle a few ministries at a time without burning out its people. The problem is that we typically try to keep ministries on life support because we have always done them or like the idea of them. That is an excellent way to keep people in a place they don't want to be and discourage them from serving more (then you will end up doing it). Let your congregation's gifts (the ones God placed in them) define what God does through your congregation instead of trying to push a square block through a round hole. God will give you what you need; just make sure you're doing what He wants.

Commitment #15 Keep Yourself Focused
on Being Instead of Just Doing

This one was hard for me to understand. I am a doer; I am constantly moving, going, producing in some way or another.

---

[36] 1 Peter 4:10 MEV

But remember, it is not about how much you do but that you are doing the right things. I, as a pastor, am called to serve God in an individual capacity. I have noticed, though, that if I focus on being who God wants me to be, I will do what God wants me to do, but if I am focused on doing what "I am supposed to do," I do not accomplish what God wants me to do. Allow Jesus to define His expectations for you, and you will never have to worry about if you have the right ones.

Being a pastor is not for the faint of heart, but one thing I would challenge you to commit to is to deal with this struggle head-on. For myself, I want to make the hard decisions and stances now that I will reap the fruit later rather than to look back on my life in regret that I didn't take a stand sooner. My kids are not getting any younger, and my wife deserves a husband. Don't allow others to determine the expectations of your ministry. You serve Jesus, so let His priorities keep your expectations in check, and you will find that ministry is a joy both at the church and in your home.

(B)

Anonymous Survey for the Church

Church Survey
For each question, please circle one response

I am a:

(Church Member) (Regular attendee) (Casual visitor) (New visitor) (Other)

1. **The environment of the church is inviting and comfortable.**

(Strongly Agree) (Agree) (Neutral) (Disagree) (Strongly Disagree)

2. **I grow from the sermons during church services.**

(Strongly Agree) (Agree) (Neutral) (Disagree) (Strongly Disagree)

3. **I feel the church has a strong direction and vision for the future.**

(Strongly Agree) (Agree) (Neutral) (Disagree) (Strongly Disagree)

4. **I am ready to embrace a vision for the future, even if it requires some change.**

(Strongly Agree) (Agree) (Neutral) (Disagree) (Strongly Disagree)

5. **I feel the church is gospel-centered.**

(Strongly Agree) (Agree) (Neutral) (Disagree) (Strongly Disagree)

6. **What would you like to see the church doing in 1 year? (please write on back)**

(C)

Leadership Covenant

———

In written acknowledgment and agreement, I
_____ hereby
sign the Leadership Covenant as stated below.

Service

- I understand that my service as a leader of _____ Church is an avenue by which I serve the Lord and will serve with excellence to the best of my ability. *(Romans 12:1,11; Matthew 23:11; Mark 10:45; 1 Peter 4:10; Colossians 3:23)*
- I covenant to serve under the headship of Christ, the authority of His Word, and the oversight of His pastor, associate pastor(s), and the other leaders in the church. *(Ephesians 4:11-16; 1 Peter 5:1-5; Hebrews 13:7-8)*
- I covenant to serve with integrity and honesty, seeking to honor the Lord in my service. *(Hebrews 13:18; Philippians 4:8; 2 Corinthians 8:21; 2 Timothy 2:15; Ephesians 4:25; James 3:17; John 6:31; 1 John 3:18)*
- I covenant to serve in my ministry in a way that aids in the larger calling to which God has called _____ Church. *(Ephesians 4:11-16; 1 Corinthians 12; Romans 15:1-6; Philippians 2:2)*

Cooperation

- I covenant to cooperate with my fellow leaders and pray for them regularly as we seek the church's best interest in following the Lord. *(1 Corinthians 12; Ephesians 4:11-16)*
- I covenant to respect my fellow leaders in the ministries that they have been called to, without undue meddling, allowing them to serve the Lord in the capacity to which He has called them. *(1 Peter 4:10)*
- I covenant to take healthy action to cooperate with the rest of the church leadership and edify the body of believers. *(Romans 12:16, 15:5-6; 1 Corinthians 1:10, 12:14-20; 2 Corinthians 13:11; Philippians 2:2; 1 Peter 3:8-9)*

Character

- I covenant that my speech will be edifying to others and used to glorify the Lord in His body. *(1 Peter 3:10-12; Ephesians 4:29; Titus 3:1-2; James 3:1-12)*
- I covenant to refrain my tongue from backbiting, gossip, and other language that may tear others down or cause division. *(2 Corinthians 12:20; Ephesians 4:29; James 1:26, 4:11; Titus 2)*
- I covenant that I will eagerly keep the unity of the Spirit in the bond of peace. This includes seeking to reconcile with those immediately I may have wronged or wronged me, watching out for divisive behavior and language, and being an avenue of peace among the body of believers. *(Ephesians 4:1-6, 32; Matthew 18:15-17; Galatians 6:1-6; James 5:19-20; 1 Corinthians 1:10; Colossians 3:13-14; 1 Peter 3:8; Hebrews 12:14; Luke 17:3; Matthew 5:23-24; Romans 12:18)*
- I covenant to keep my lifestyle as an example to the believers in speech, conduct, love, spirit, faith, and purity. *(1 Timothy 4:12)*

Reconciliation

- I covenant to follow the reconciliation process both for personal reconciliation or in aiding others, as found in Matthew 18:15-17 to seek reconciliation privately, then with witnesses and ultimately before the church. *(Matthew 18:15-17)*
- I covenant to keep my fellow leaders accountable to legal, biblical, moral, and ethical guidelines, and this covenant to keep the church's reputation clean and honest. *(2 Corinthians 6:3; Jude 12-13; 1 Peter 2:11-17,4:15-17)*

Name: _____ Date: _____